HISTORY

OF THE

WAR IN SOUTH AFRICA

1899–1902

COMPILED BY DIRECTION OF
HIS MAJESTY'S GOVERNMENT

BY

MAJOR-GENERAL SIR FREDERICK MAURICE, K.C.B.

WITH A STAFF OF OFFICERS

MAPS • VOLUME I

The Naval & Military Press Ltd

Published by
The Naval & Military Press Ltd
5 Riverside, Brambleside, Bellbrook
Industrial Estate, Uckfield, East Sussex,
TN22 1QQ England
Tel: +44 (0) 1825 749494
Fax: +44 (0) 1825 765701
www.naval-military-press.com

In reprinting in facsimile from the original, any imperfections are inevitably reproduced and the quality may fall short of modern type and cartographic standards.

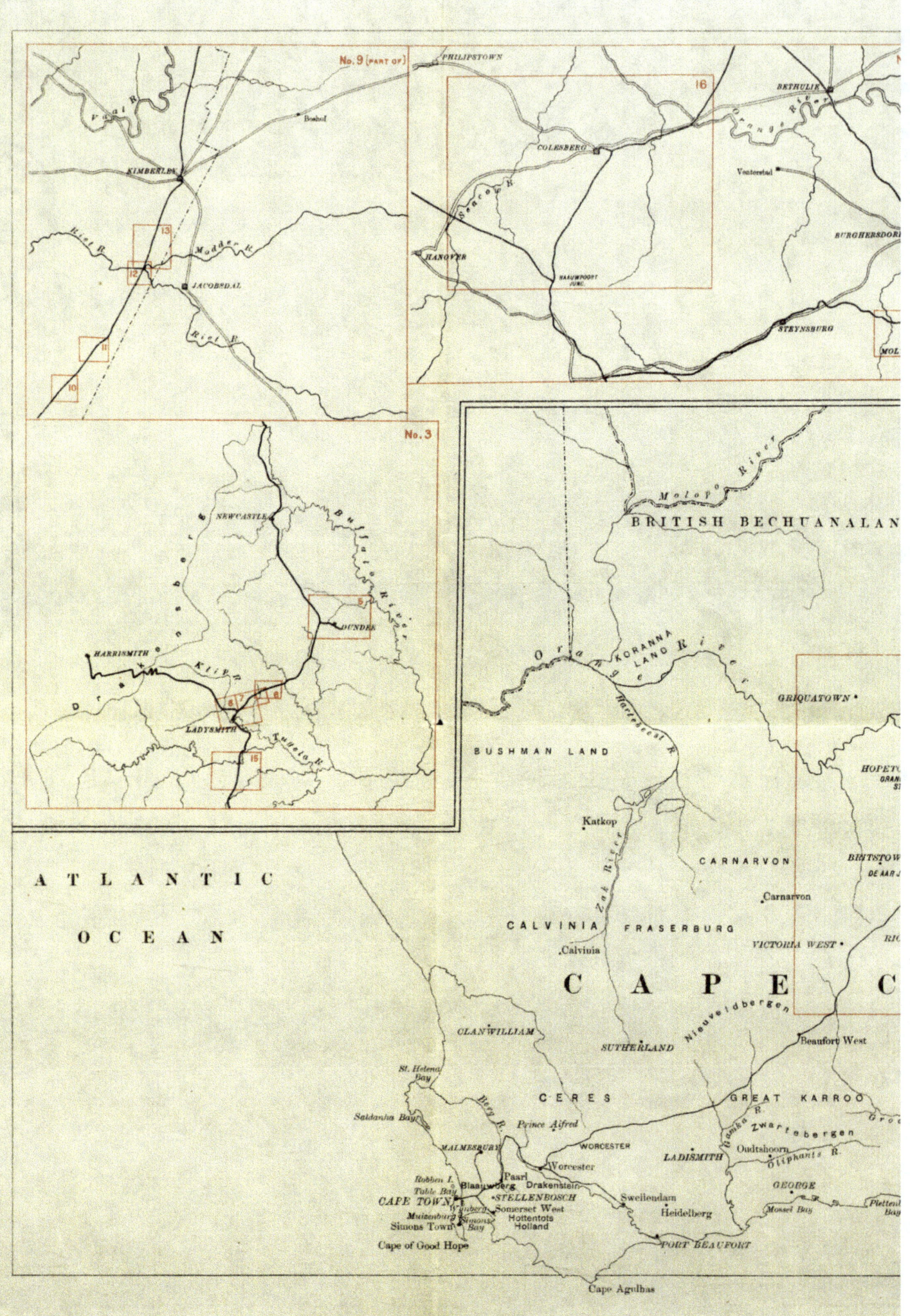

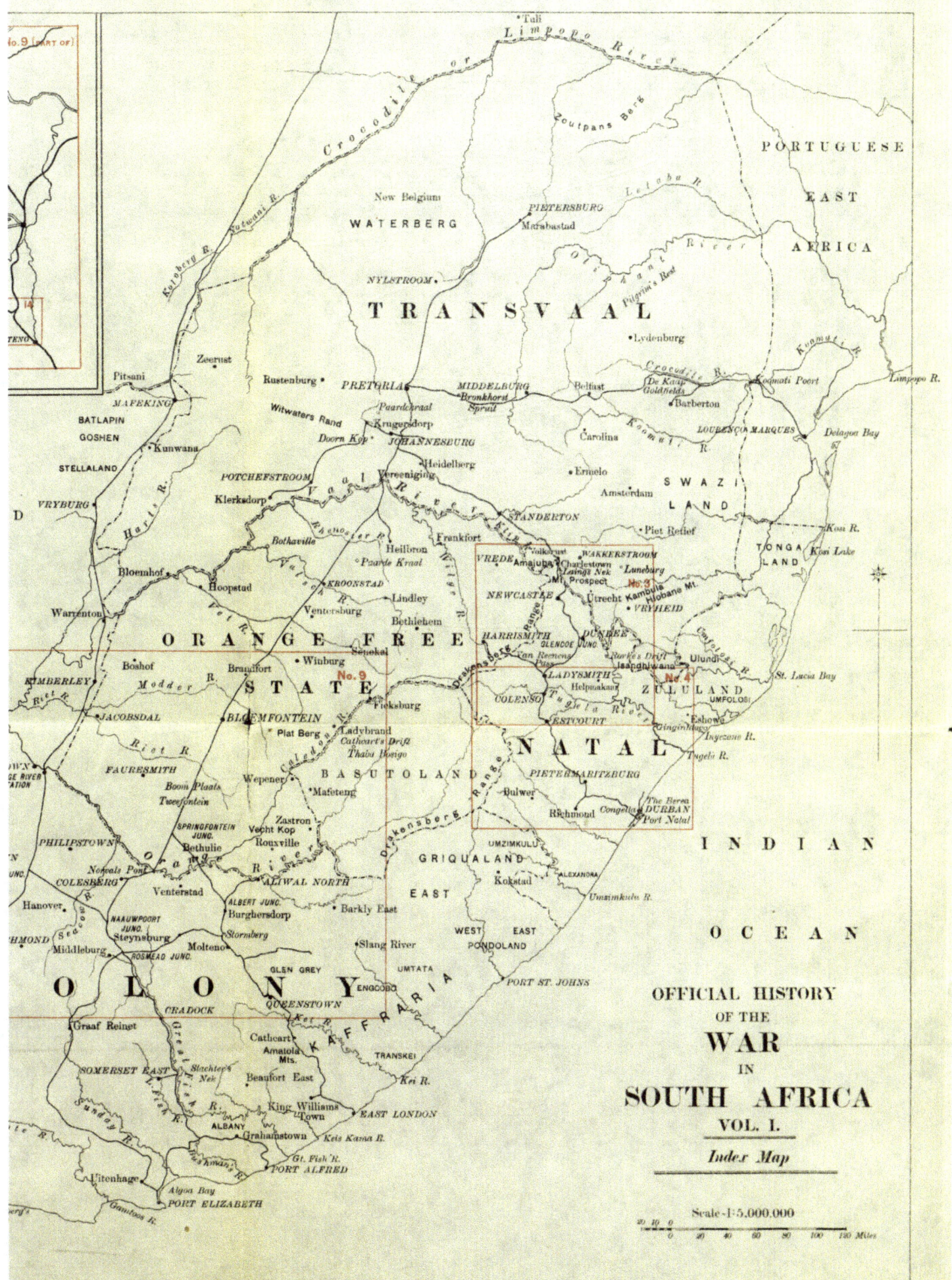

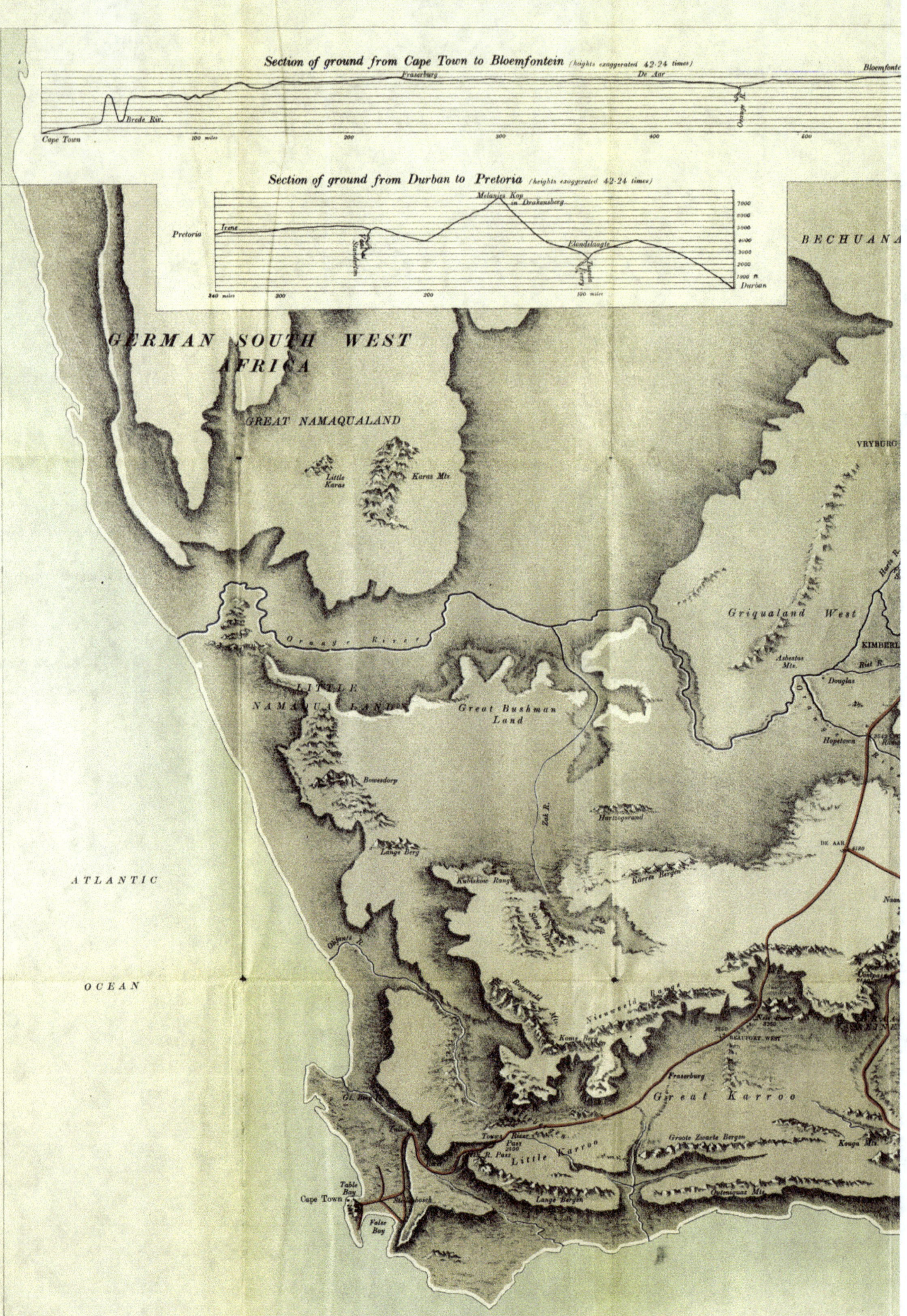

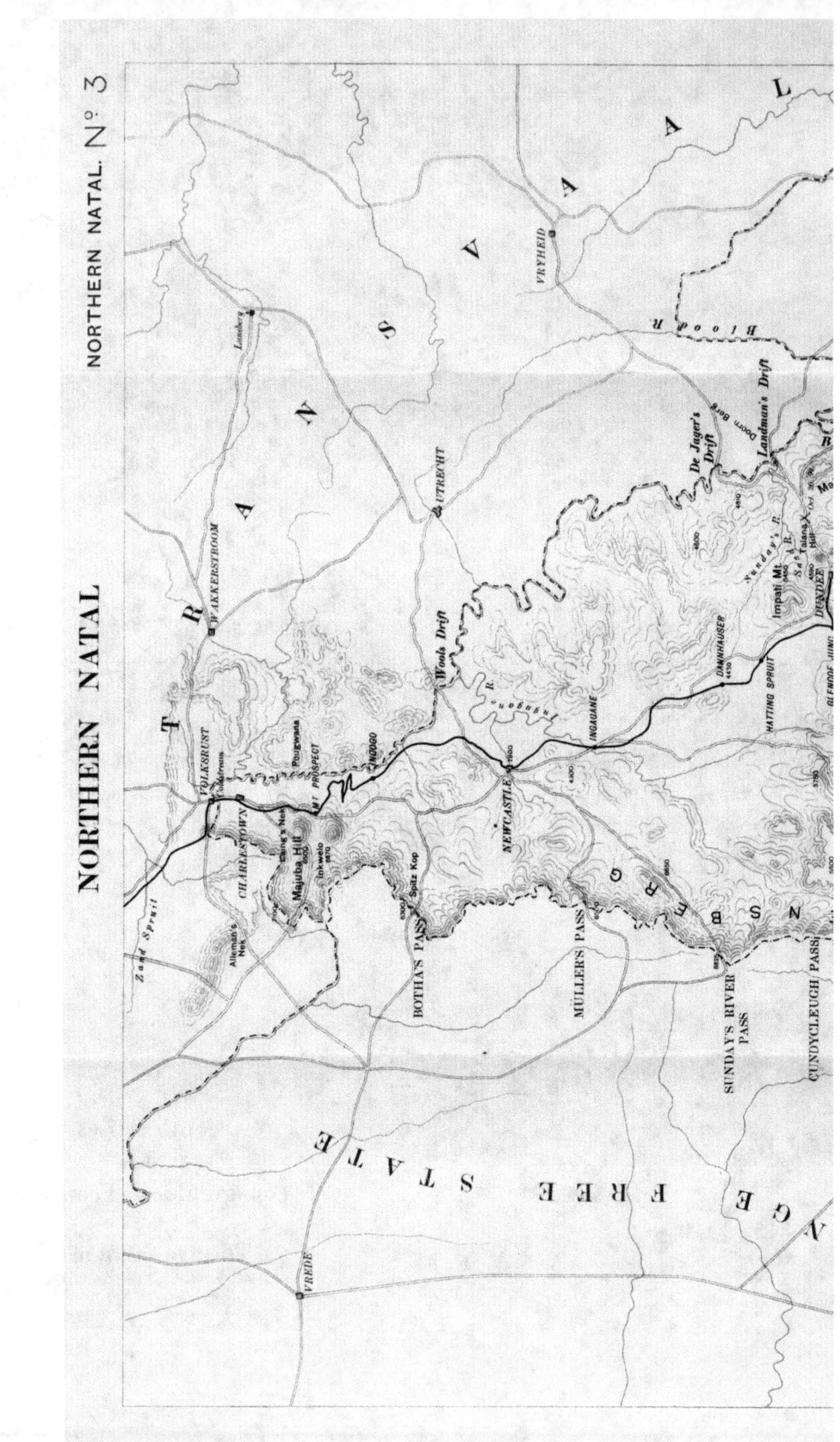

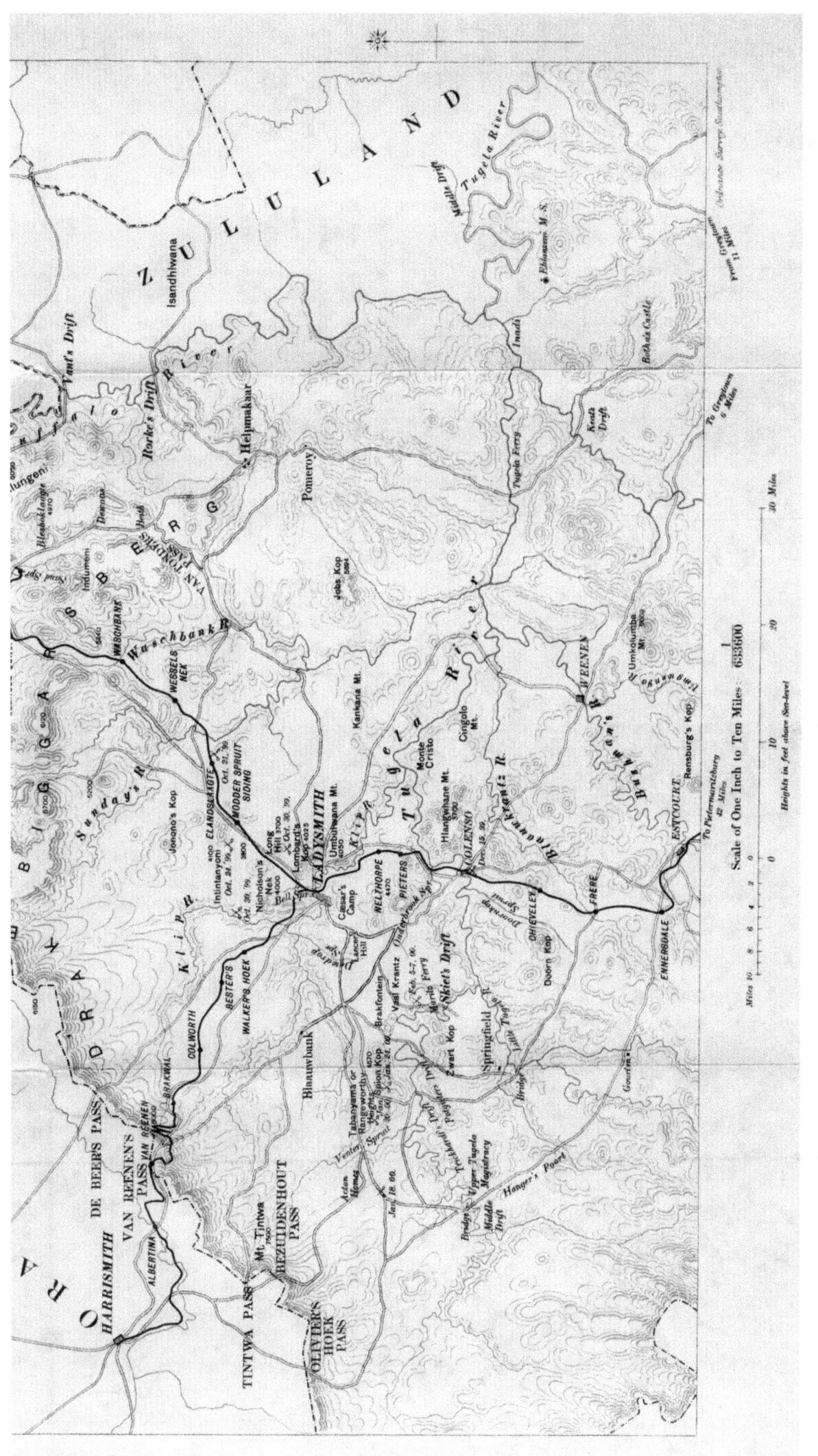

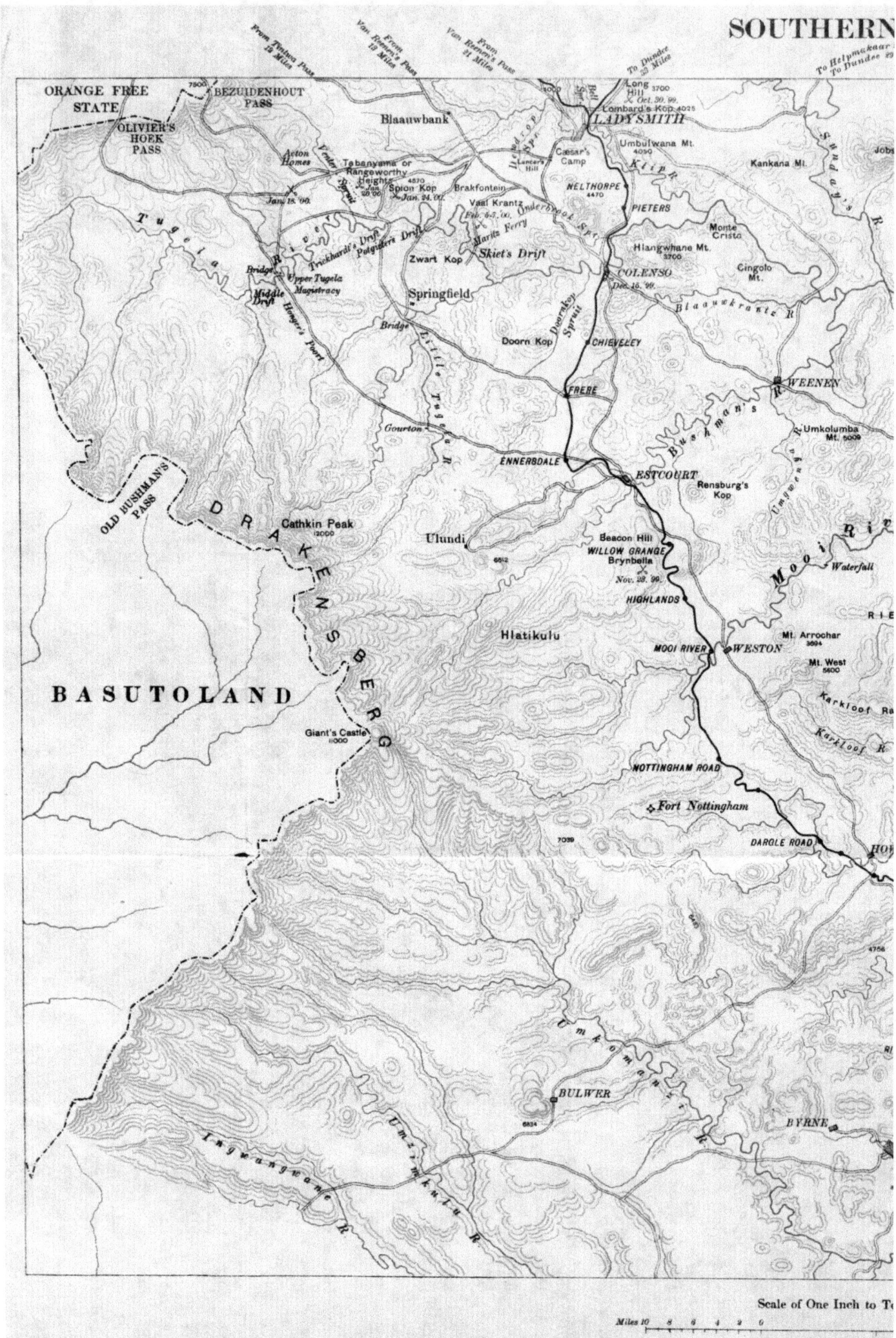

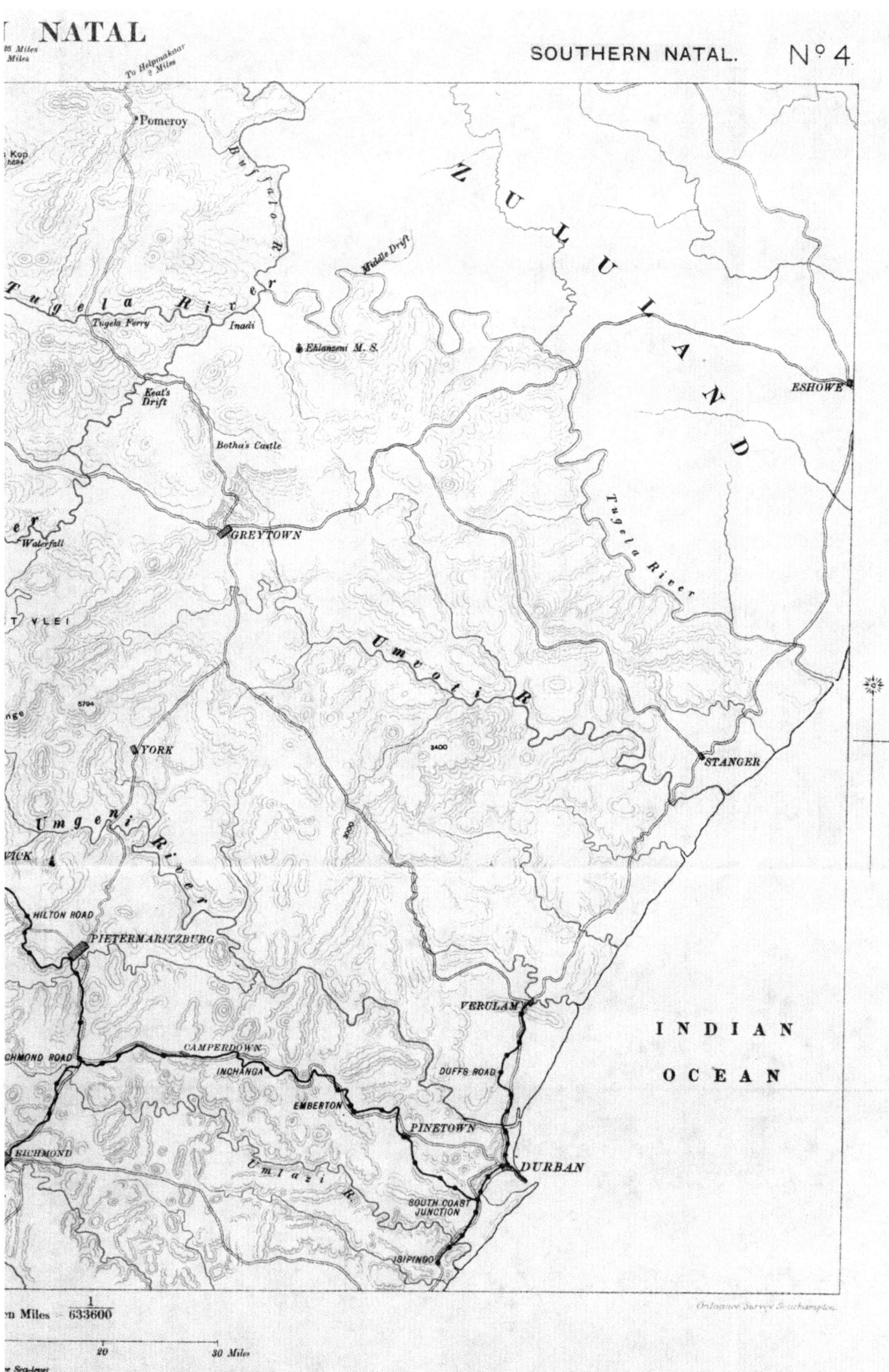

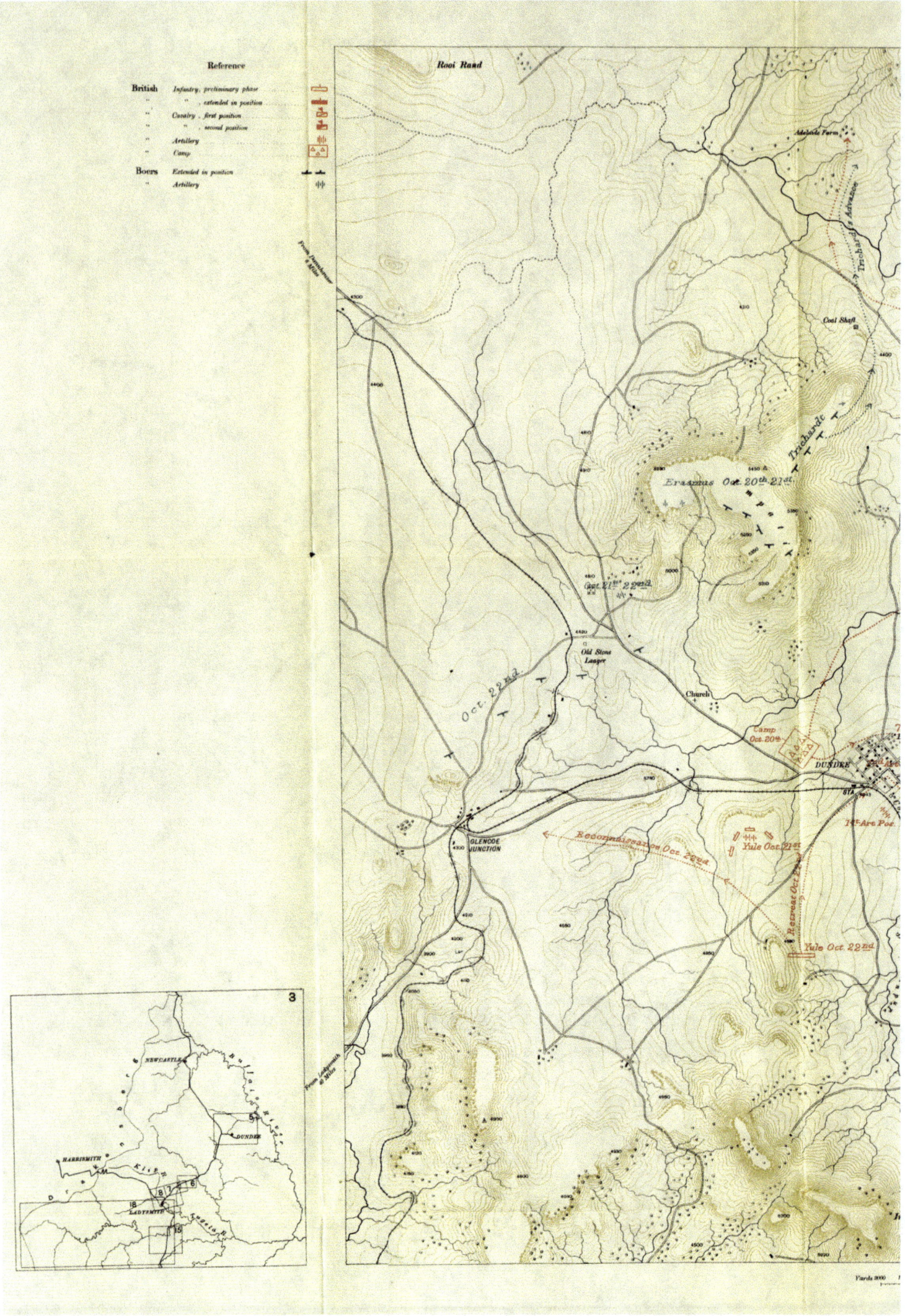

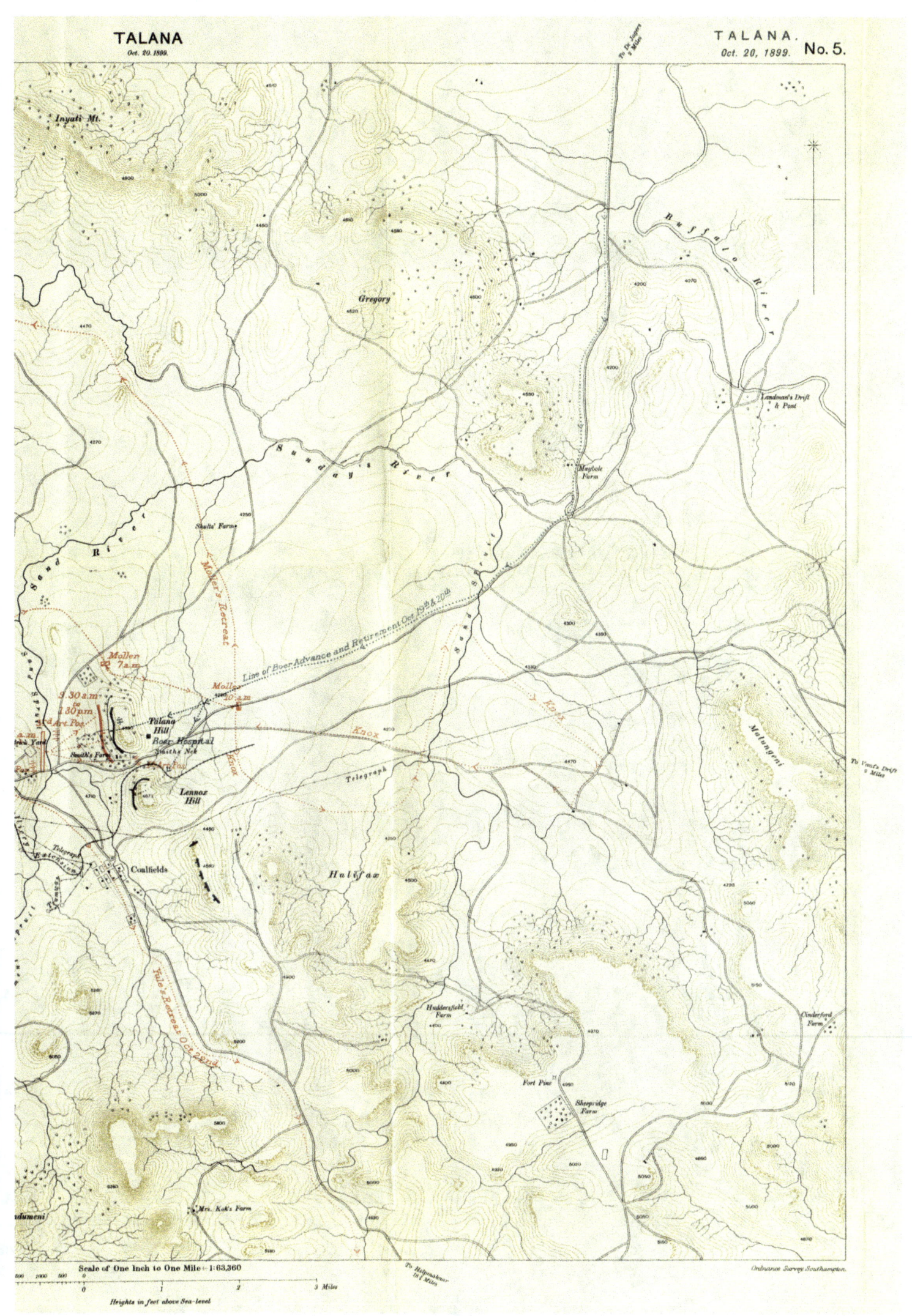

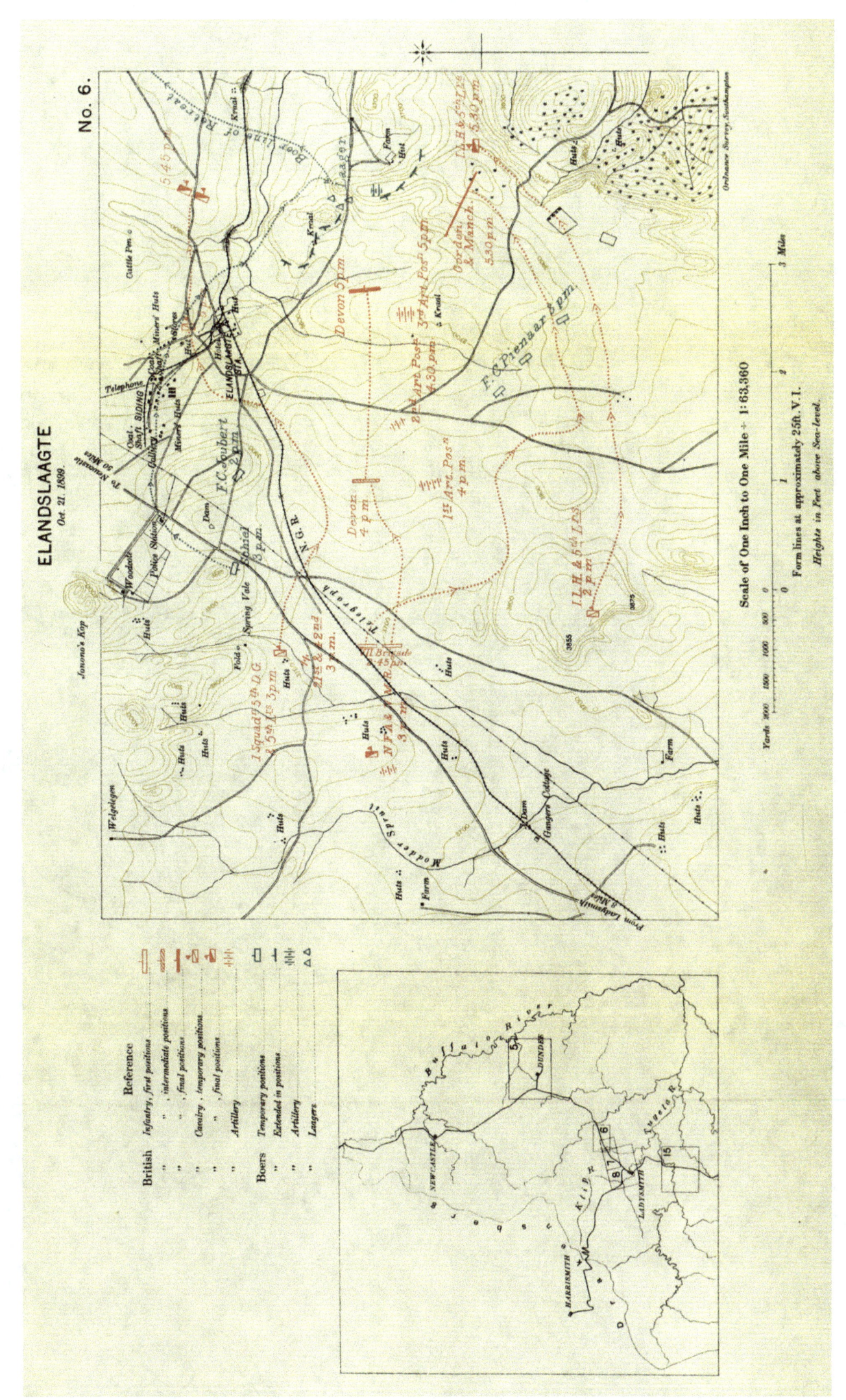

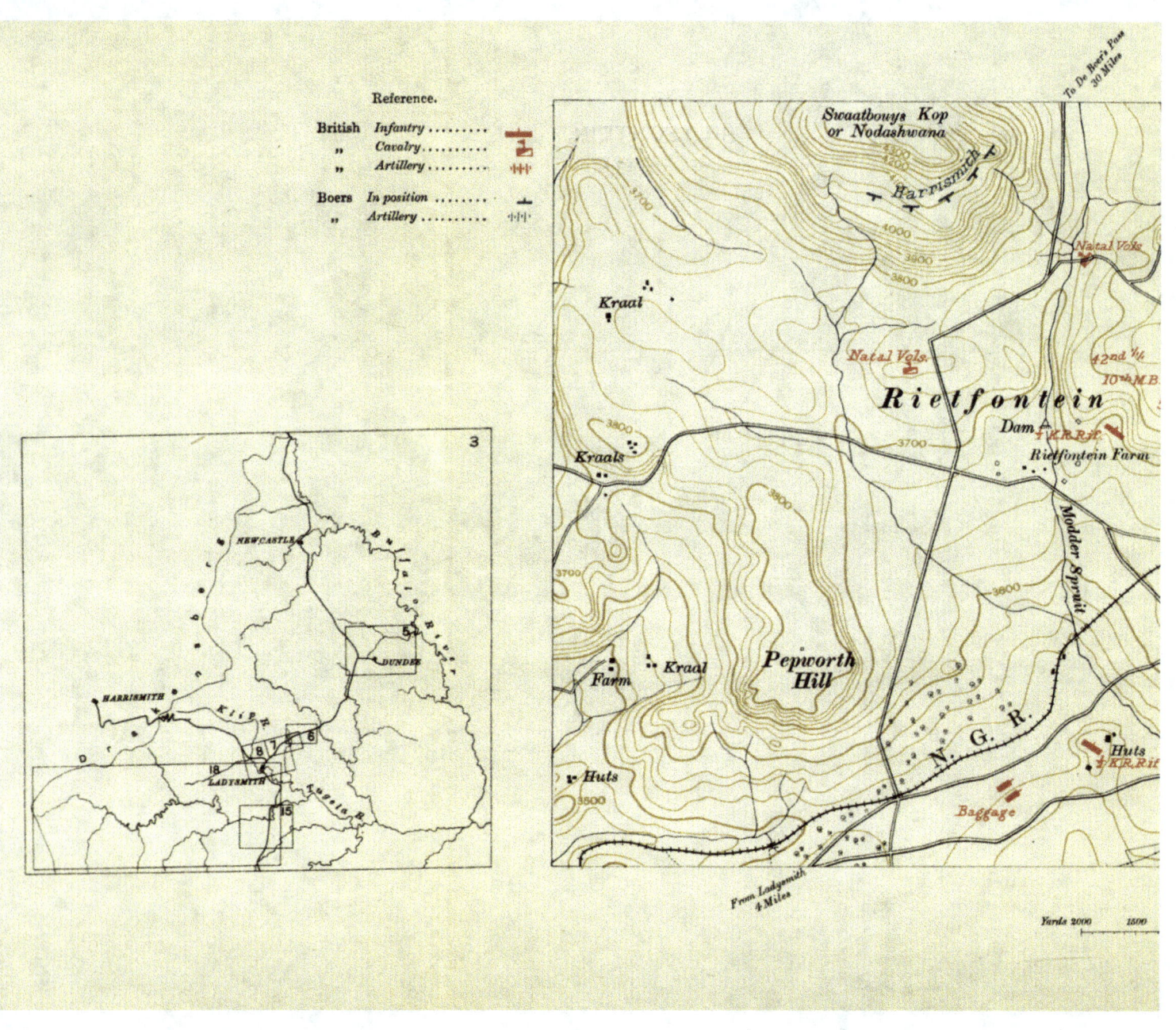

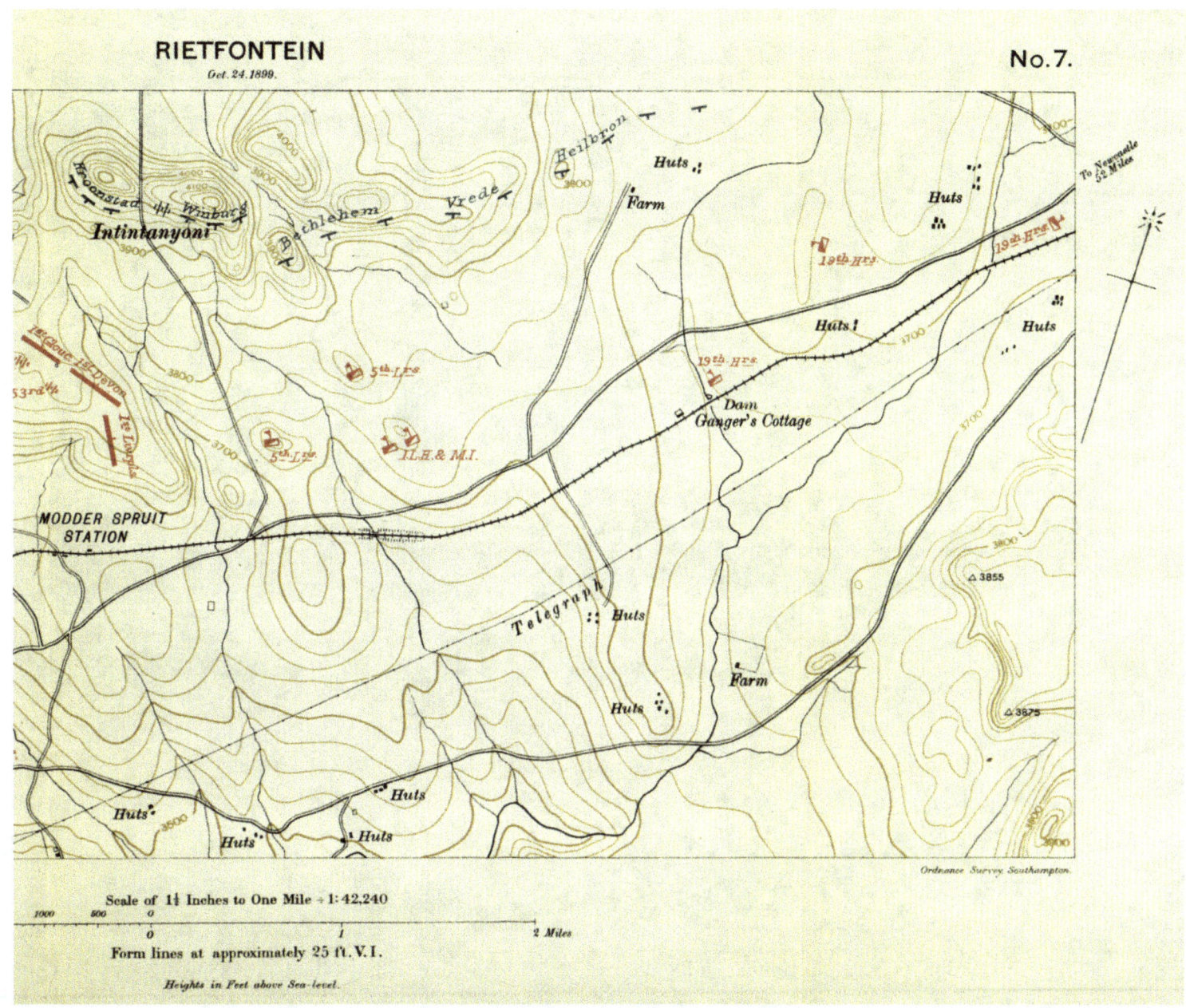

Reference

British Infantry
" Cavalry
" Artillery
Boers
" Extended in position
" Artillery

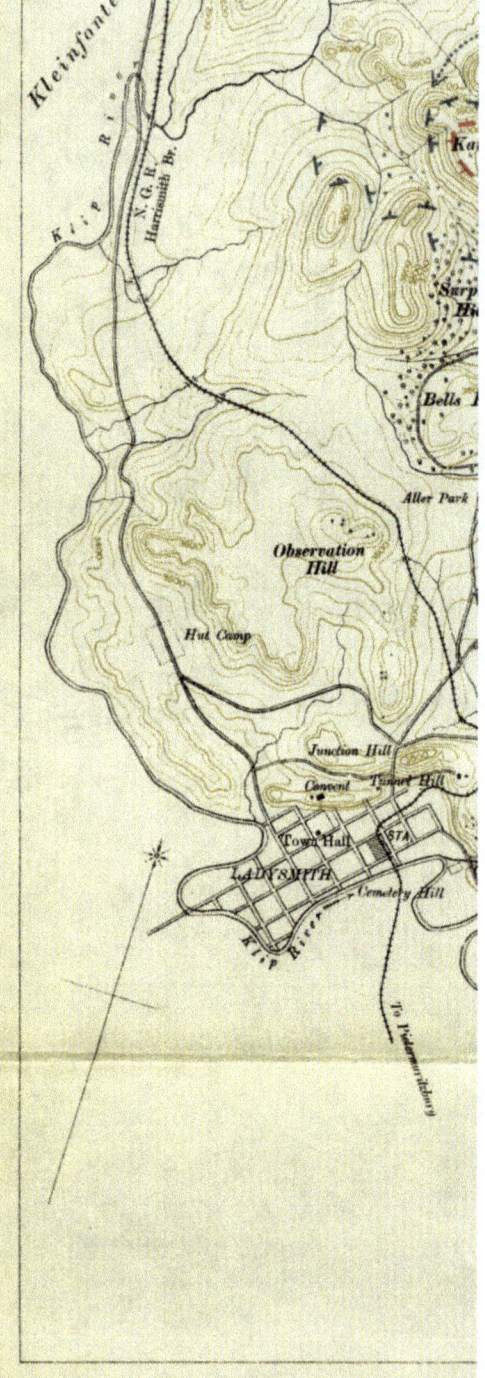

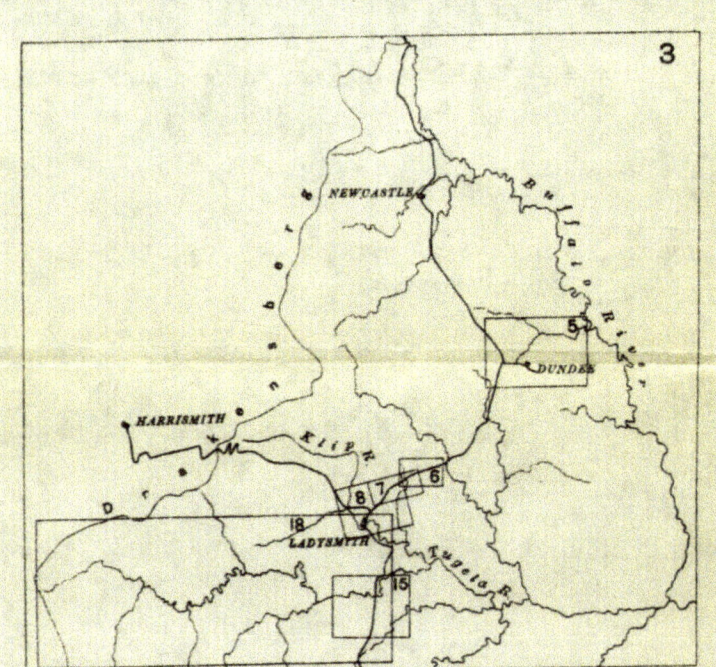

Reference

British Infantry
" Cavalry
" Artillery
Boers
" Extended in position
" Artillery

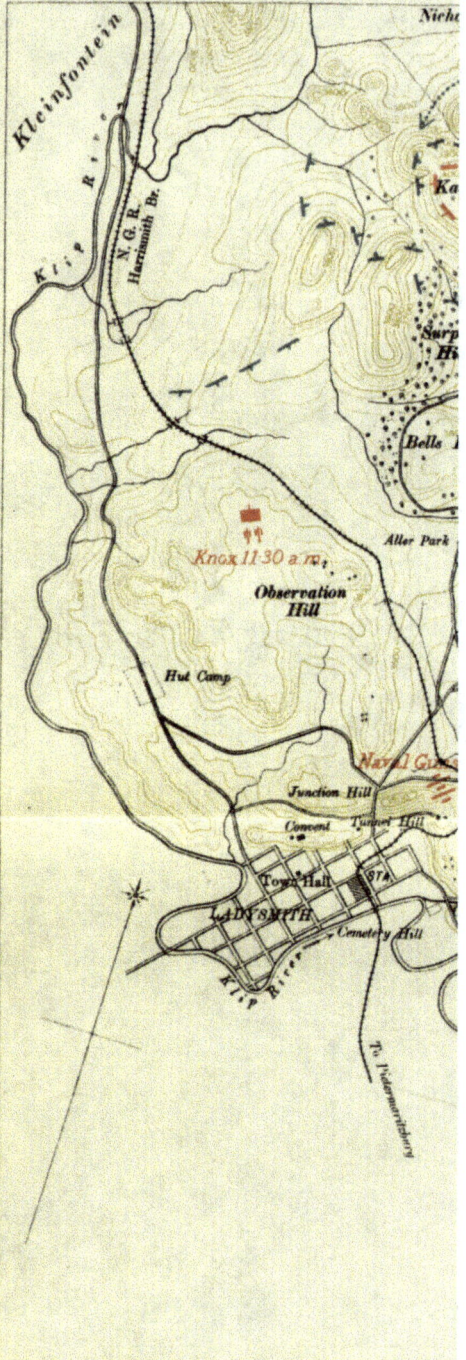

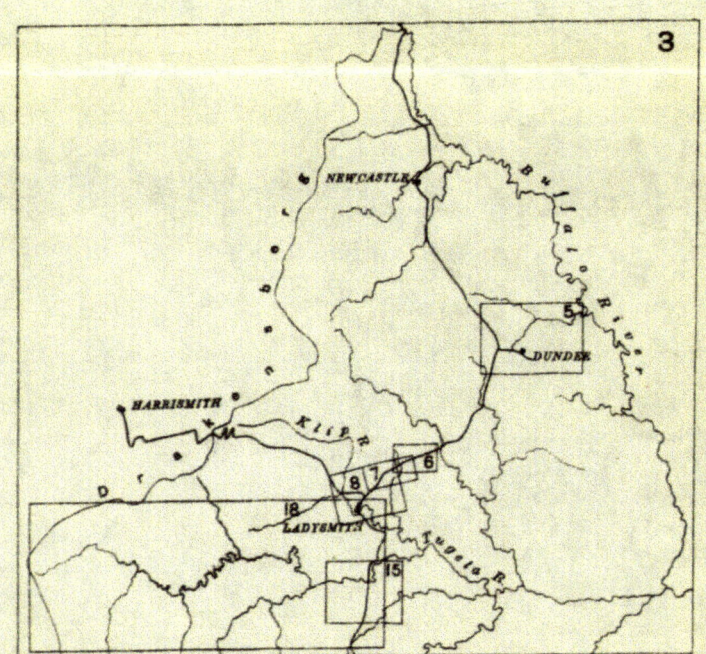

LOMBARDS KOP
Oct. 30. 1899.

SITUATION FROM 7. A.M. TO CLOSE OF ACTION

No. 8.(a)

Scale of 1 Inch to 2000 Yards = 1:72,000

Form lines at approximately 25 ft. V.I.
Heights in feet above Sea-level.

Ordnance Survey Southampton

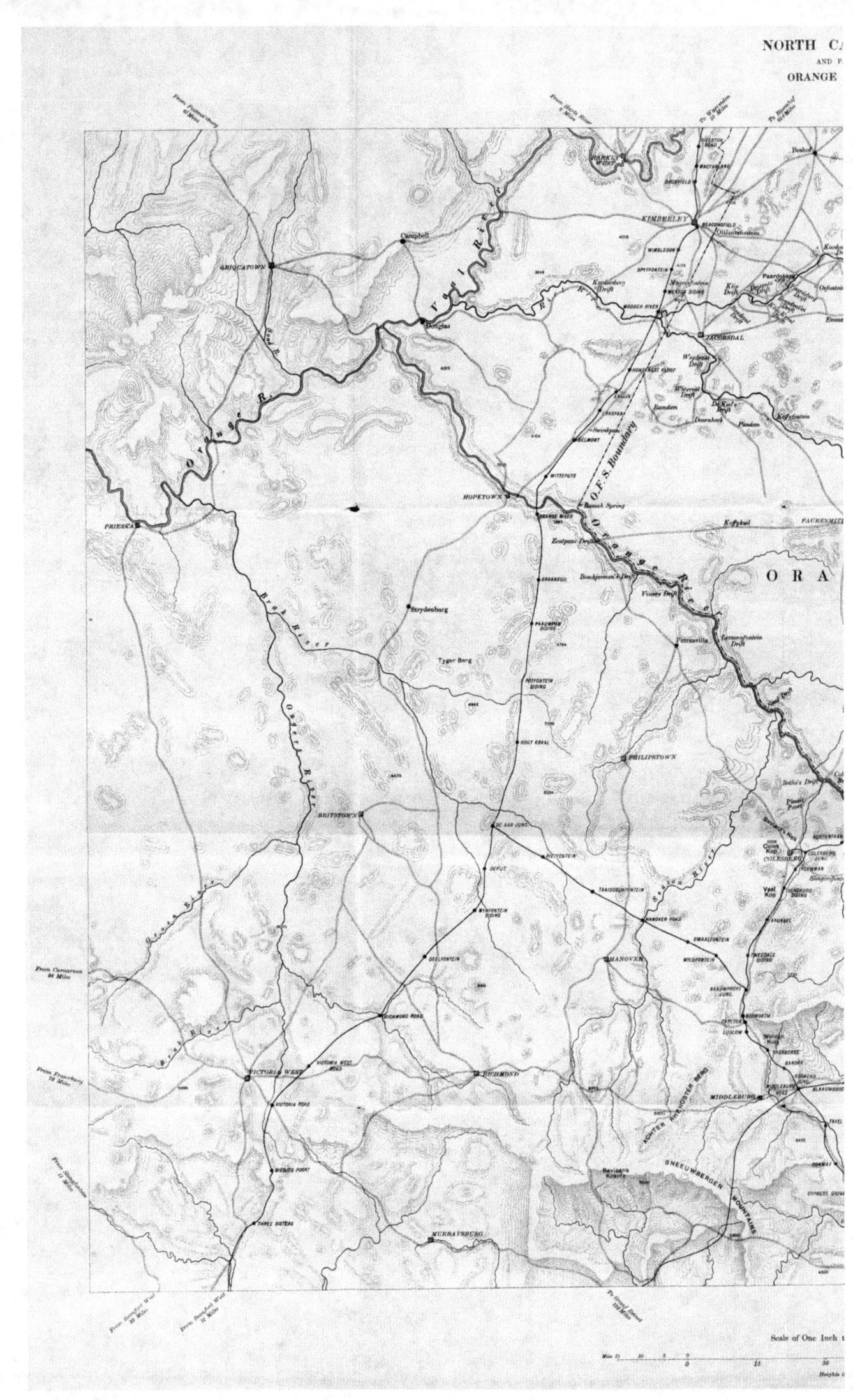

CAPE COLONY
PART OF THE
FREE STATE

No. 9.

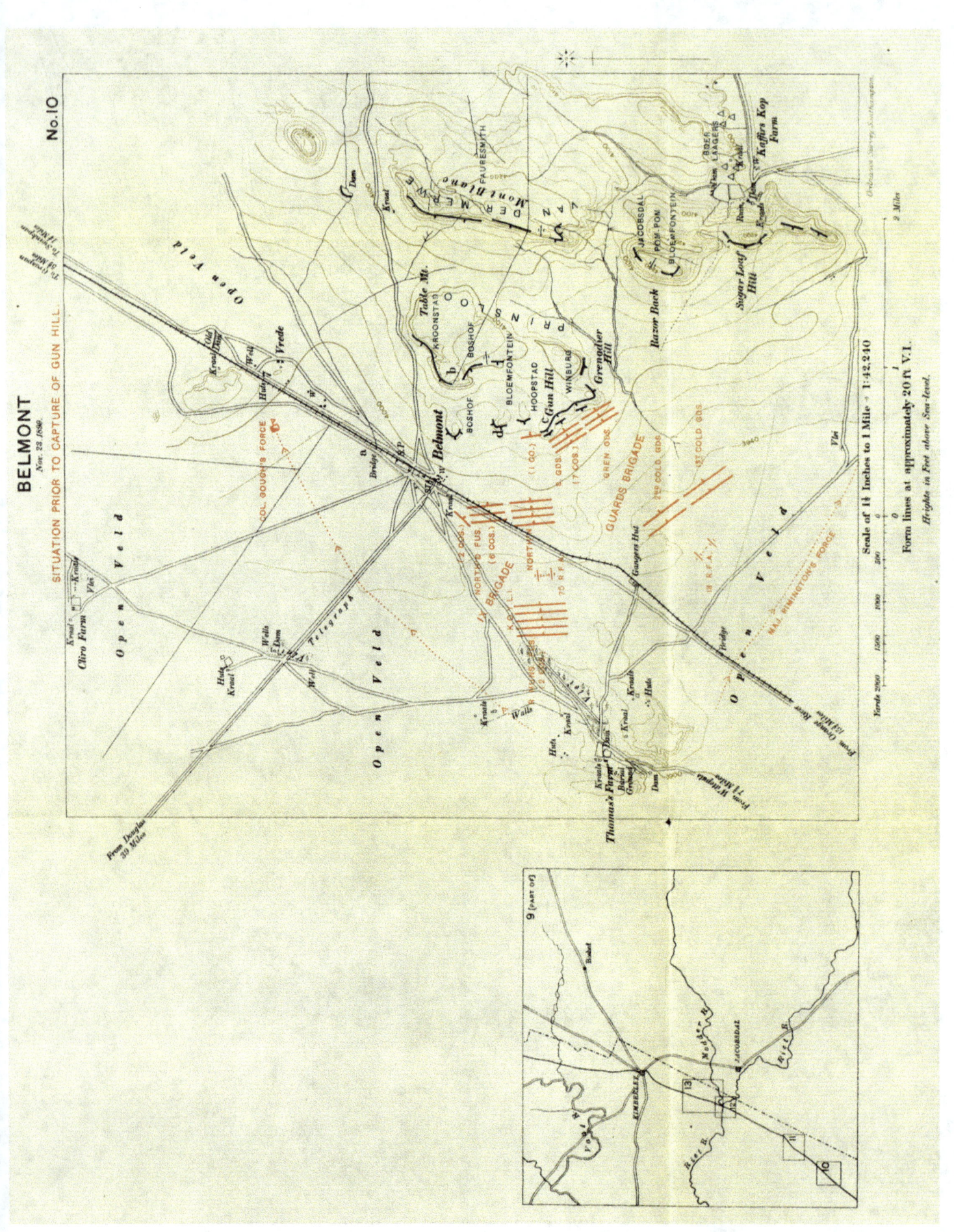

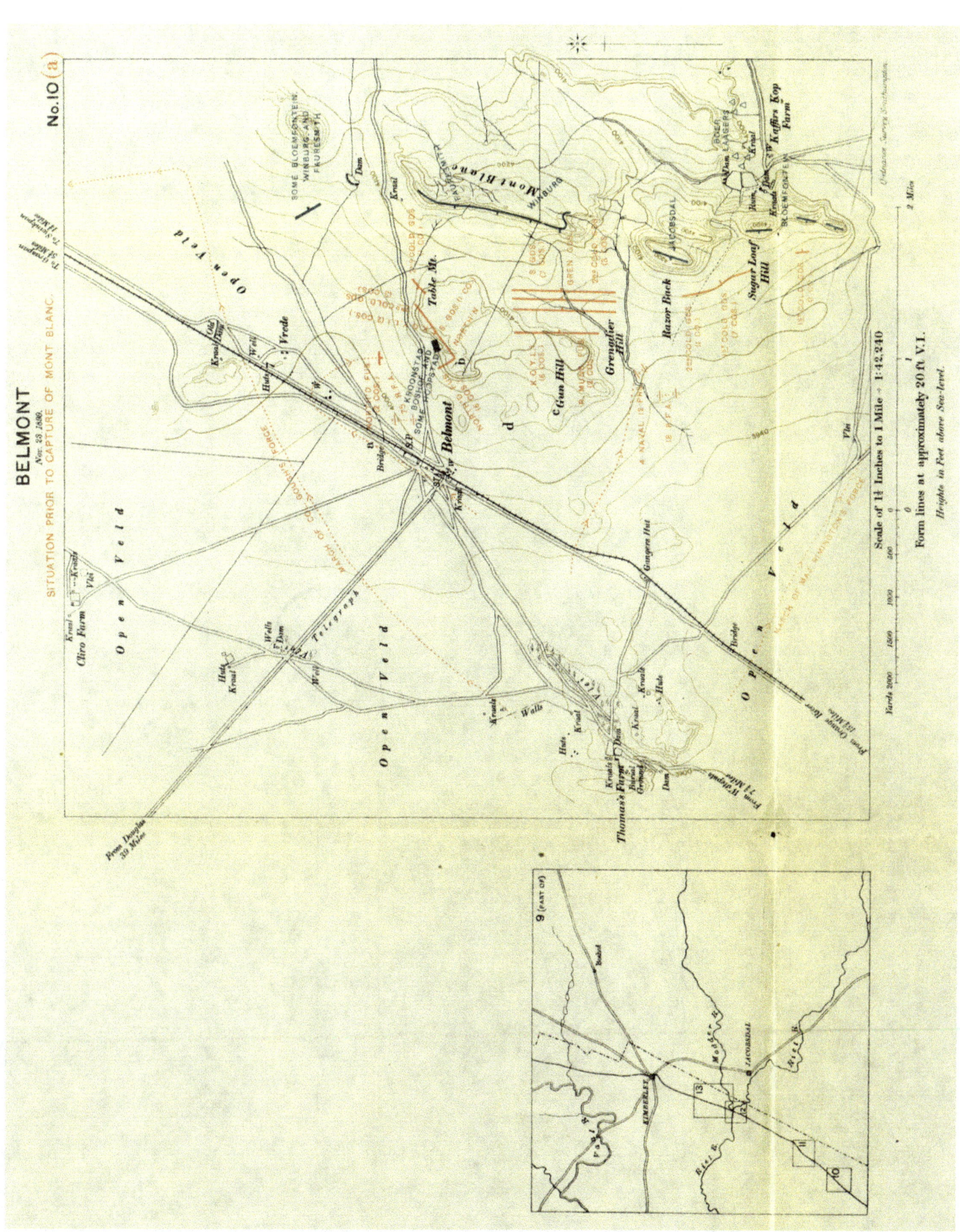

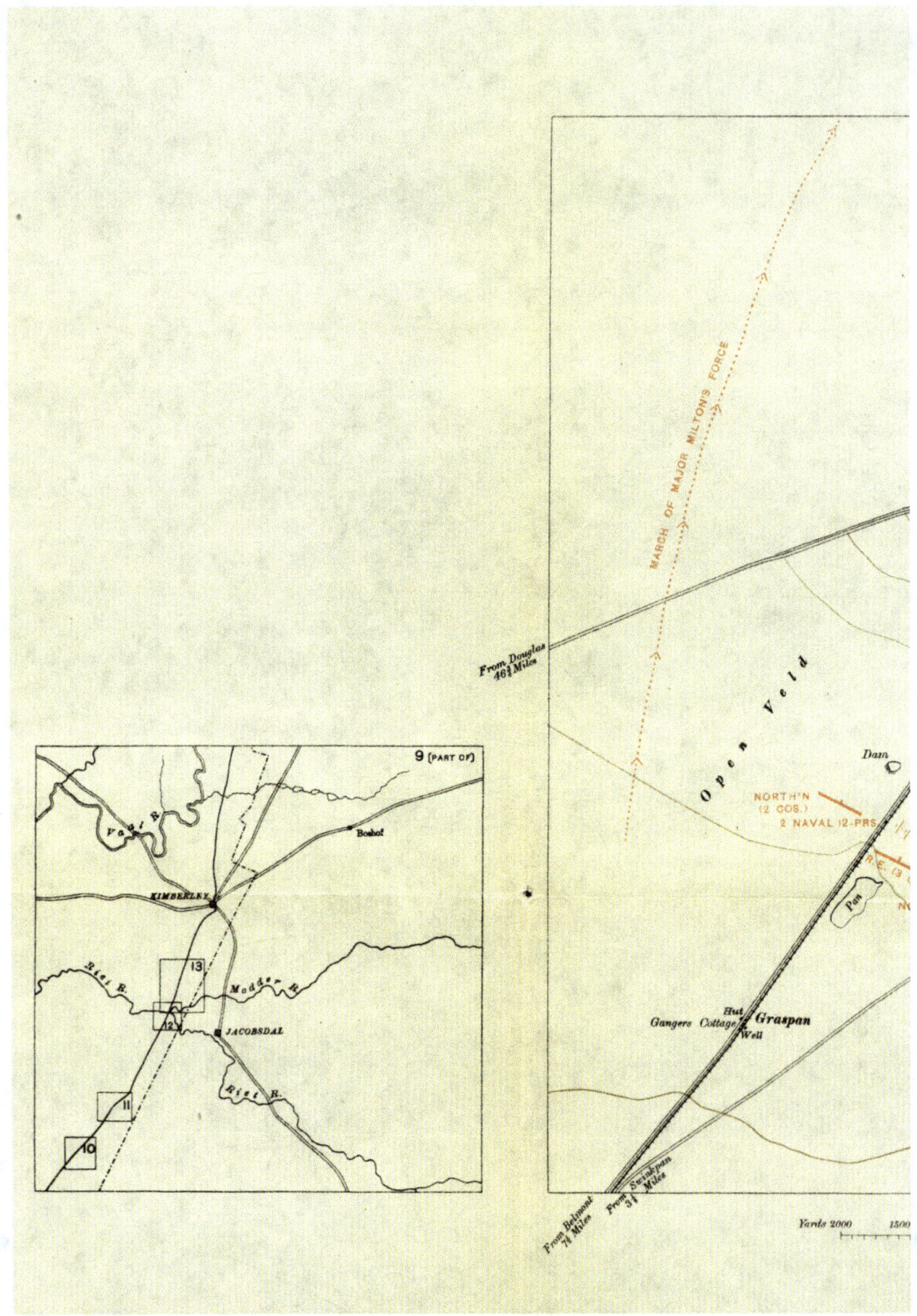

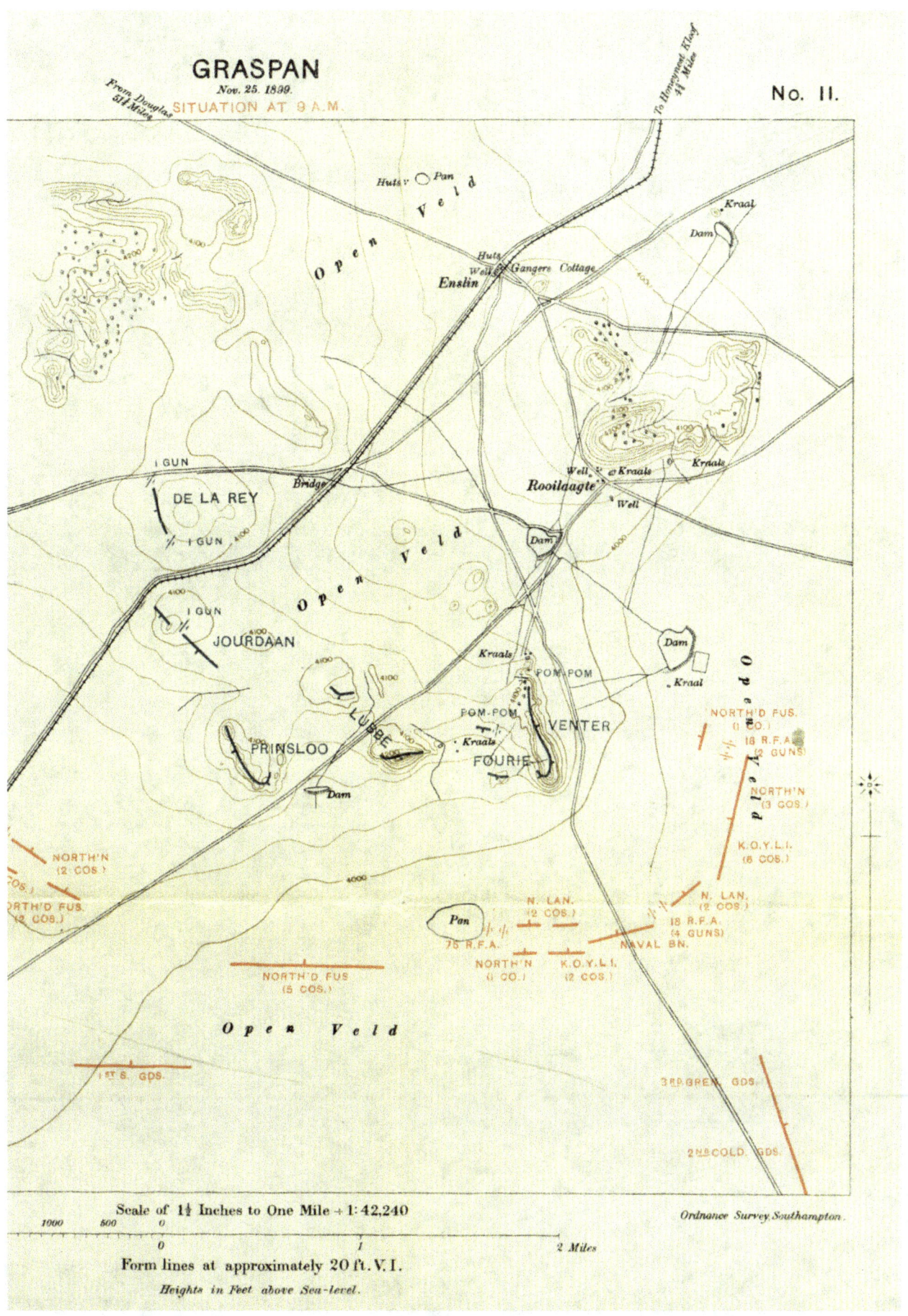

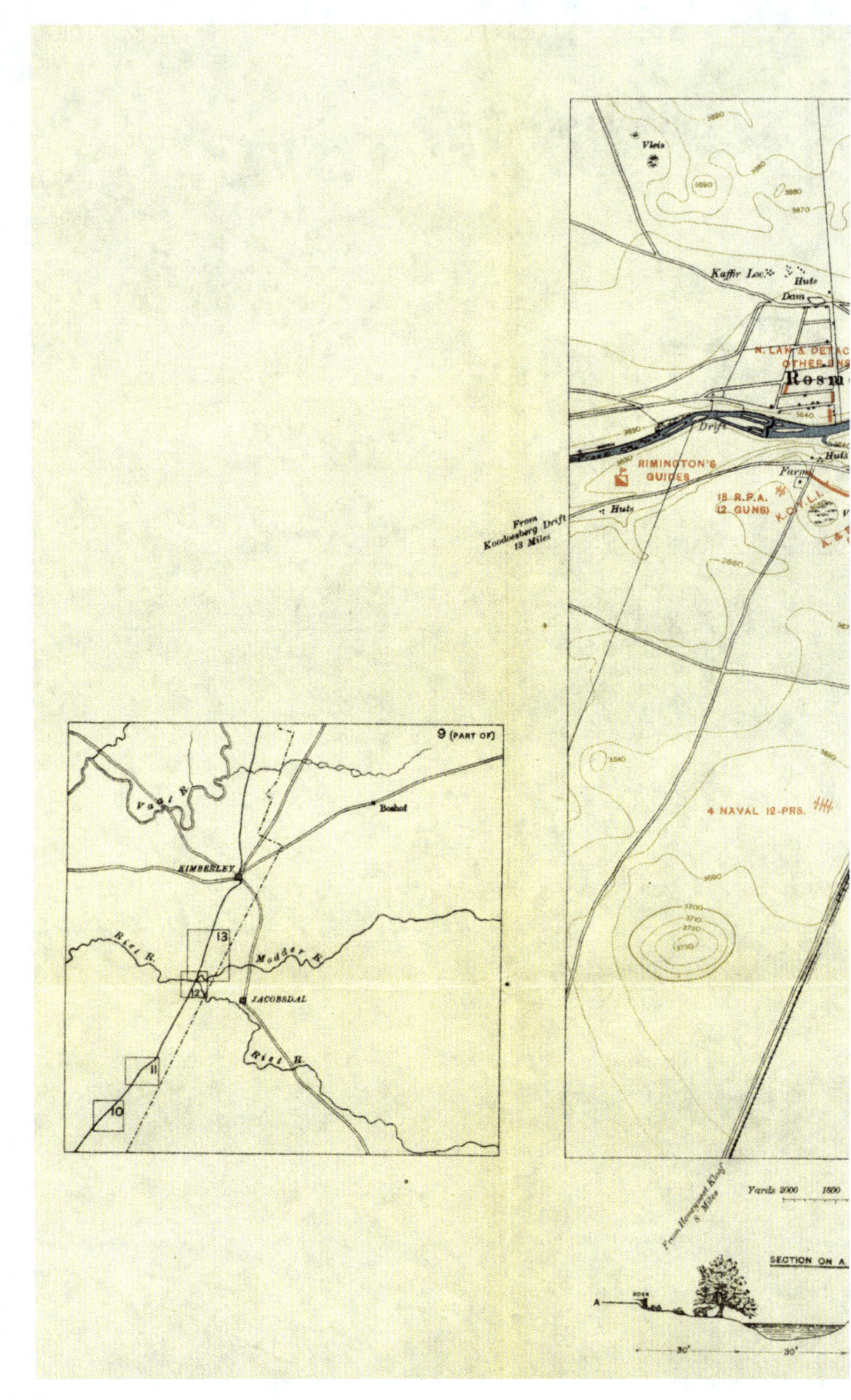

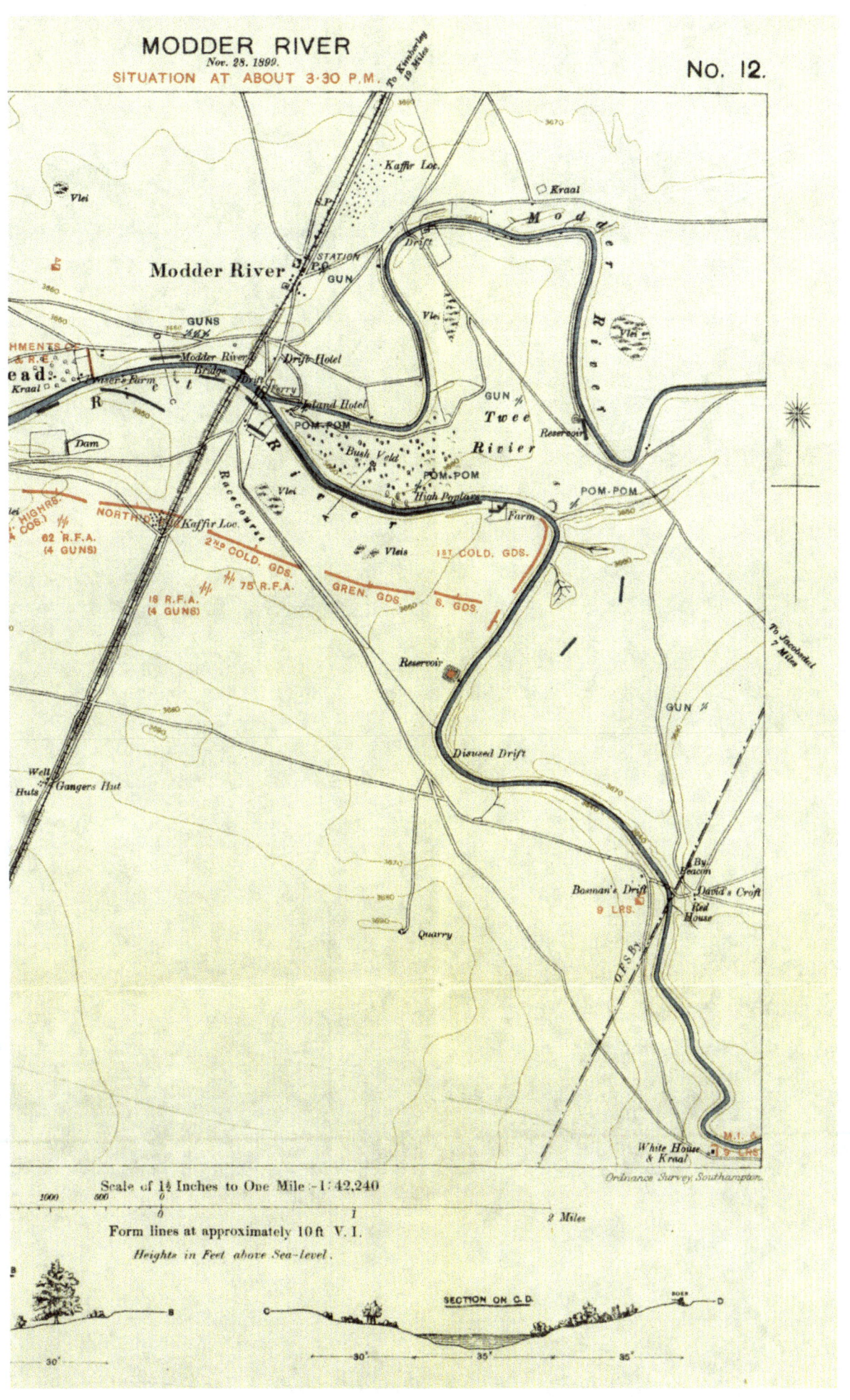

9 (PART OF)
Vaal R.
Boshof
KIMBERLEY
Riet R.
Modder R.
13
12
JACOBSDAL
Riet R.
11
10

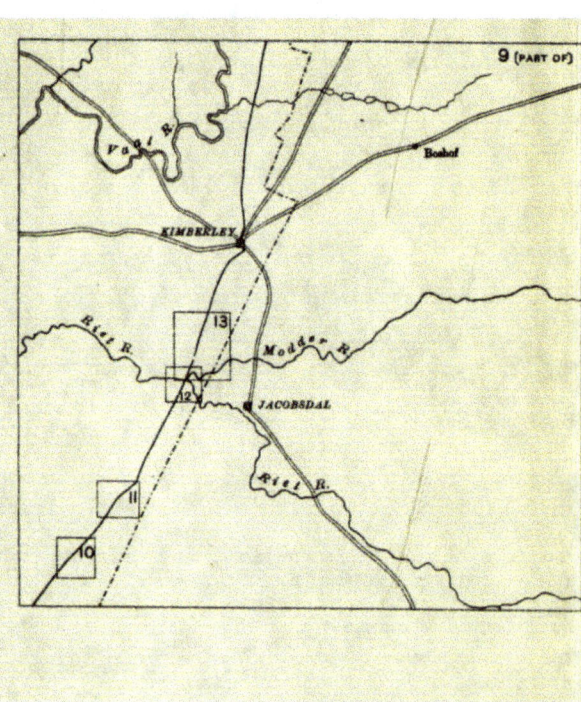

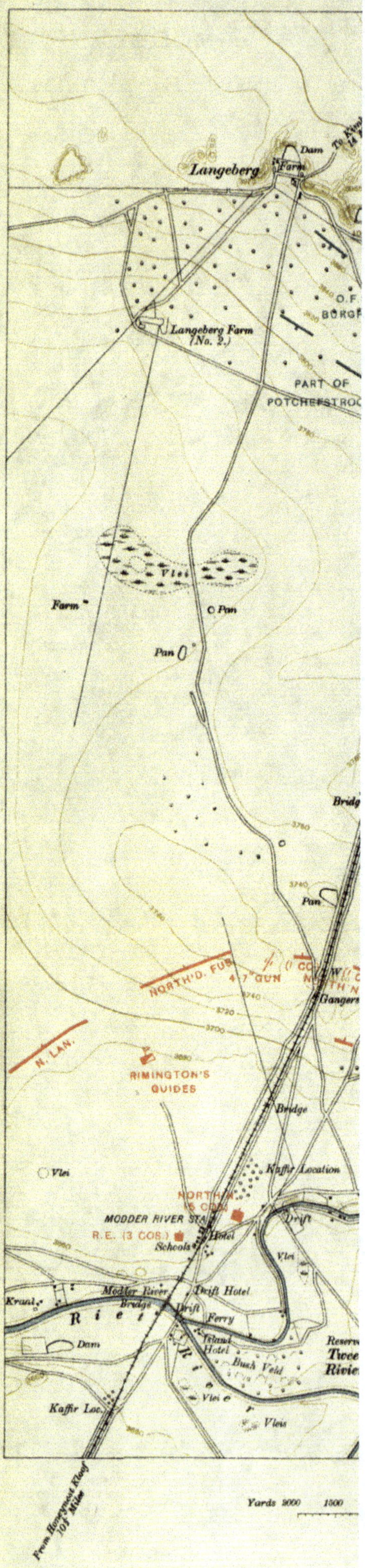
Langeberg
Dam
Farm
Langeberg Farm (No. 2.)
Vlei
Farm
Pan
Pan
NORTH'D. FUS.
4·7 GUN
Gangers
N. LAN.
RIMINGTON'S GUIDES
Bridge
Kaffir Location
Vlei
MODDER RIVER STA.
R.E. (3 COS.)
Schools
Hotel
Drift
Vlei
Kraal
Modder River Bridge
Drift Hotel
Drift
Riet
Ferry
Dam
Island Hotel
Bush Veld
Kaffir Loc.
Vlei
Vleis
Yards 2000 1500
From Honeynest Kloof 10½ Miles

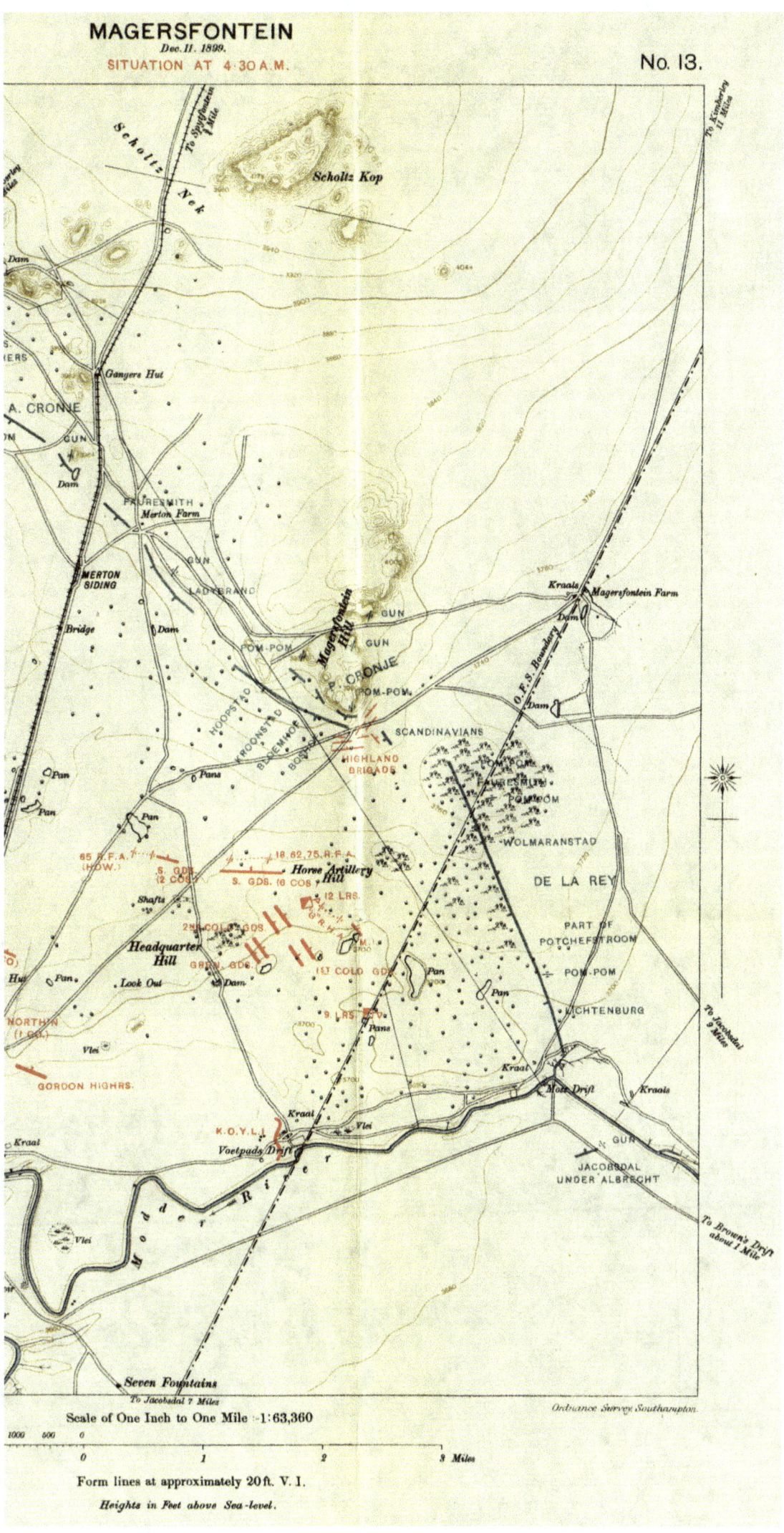

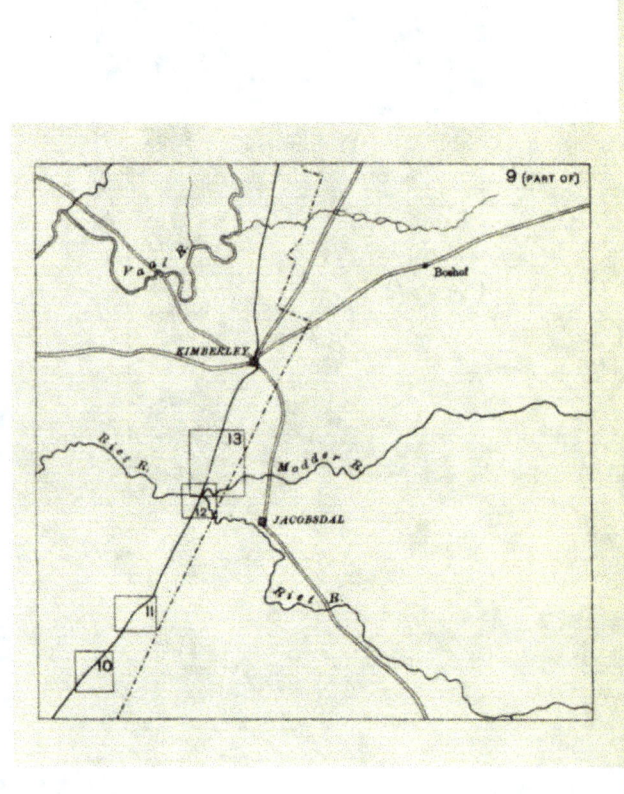
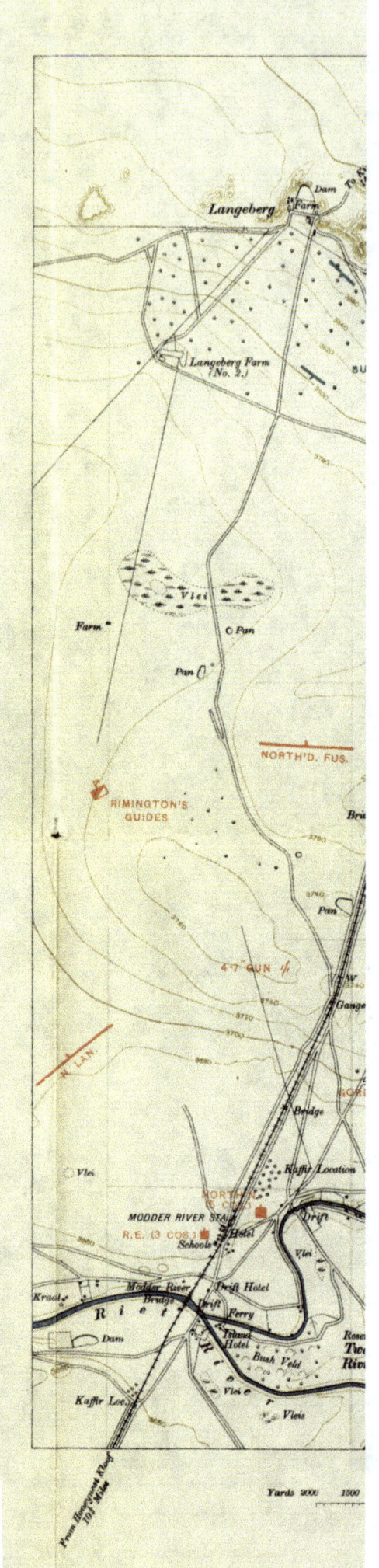

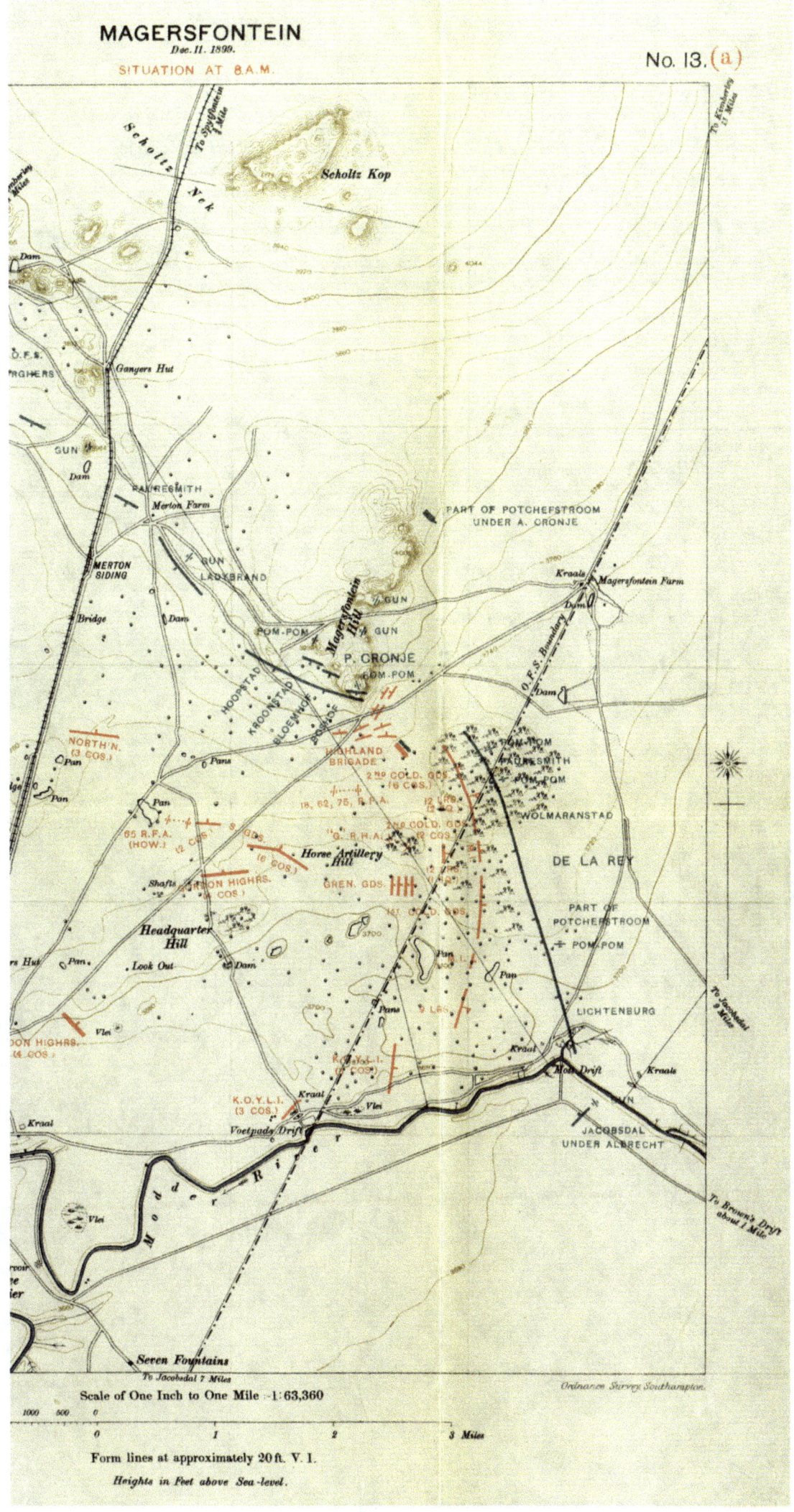

9 [PART OF]
14
MOLTENO
BURGHERSDORP
BETHULIE
Orange River
STEYNSBURG
24
16
COLESBERG
NAAUWPOORT JUNC.
HANOVER
PHILIPSTOWN

Dam
Bamboo Spruit
Dam
From Steynsberg
C. G. R.
(Midland Section)
Dam
House
STEINKAMP
GROBELAAR
Oudeklip
Rietpoort Berg
Hartebeeste Nek
House
J. Roberts
From Marais berg
Vaal Kop
House
Van Zyls
Bamboosberg Spruit
Cape Collieries Railway
House
House
House
Dam
Zevenfontein
From Cape Collieries
D. P. Van Zyls
Yards 2000 1500

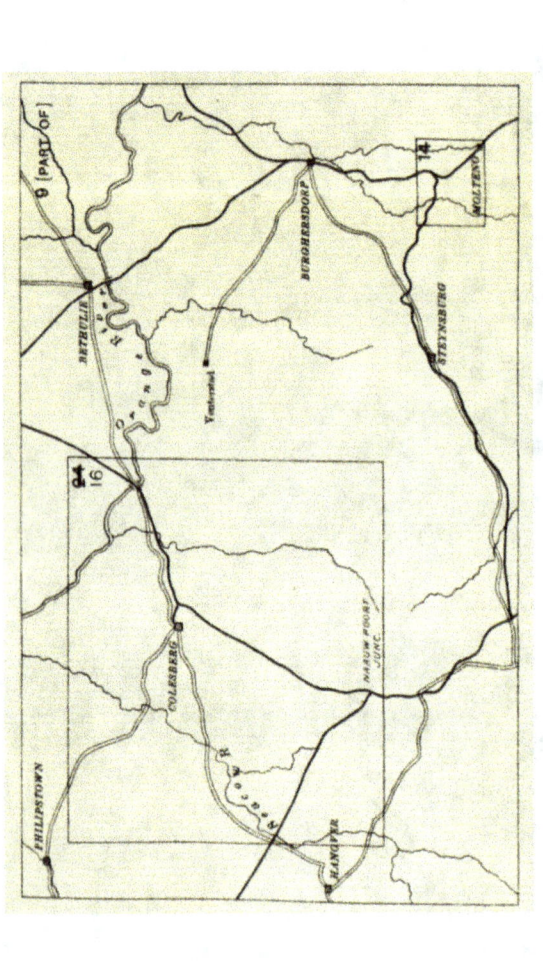

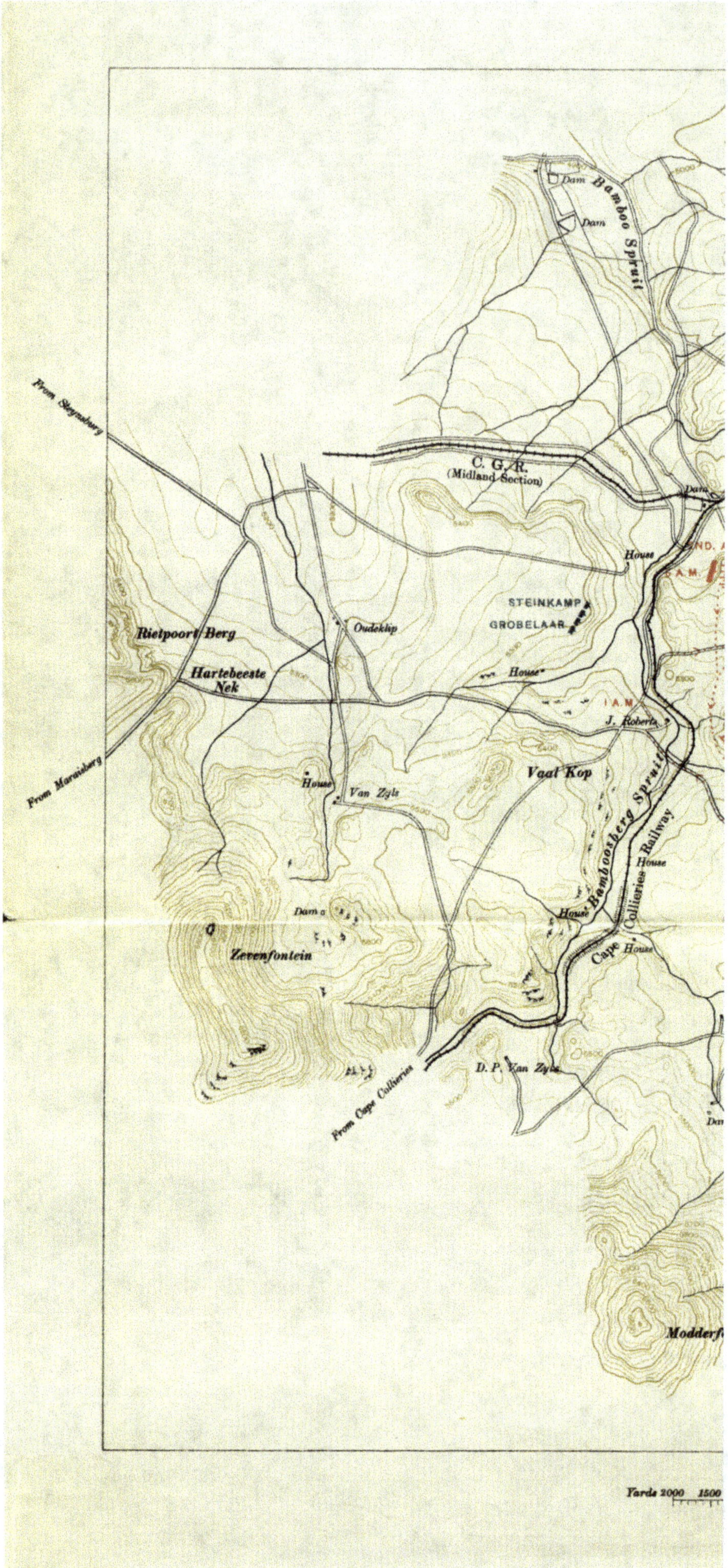

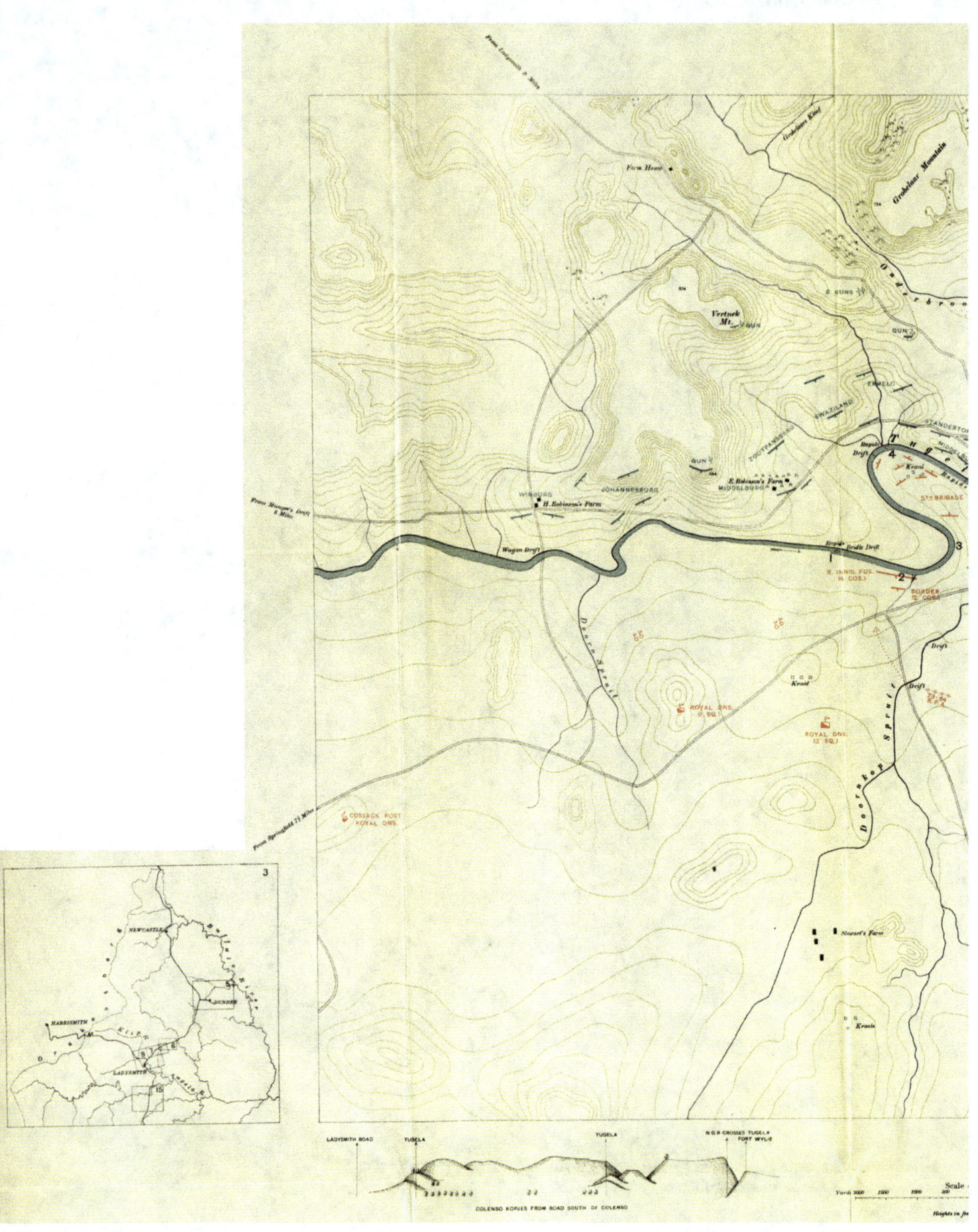

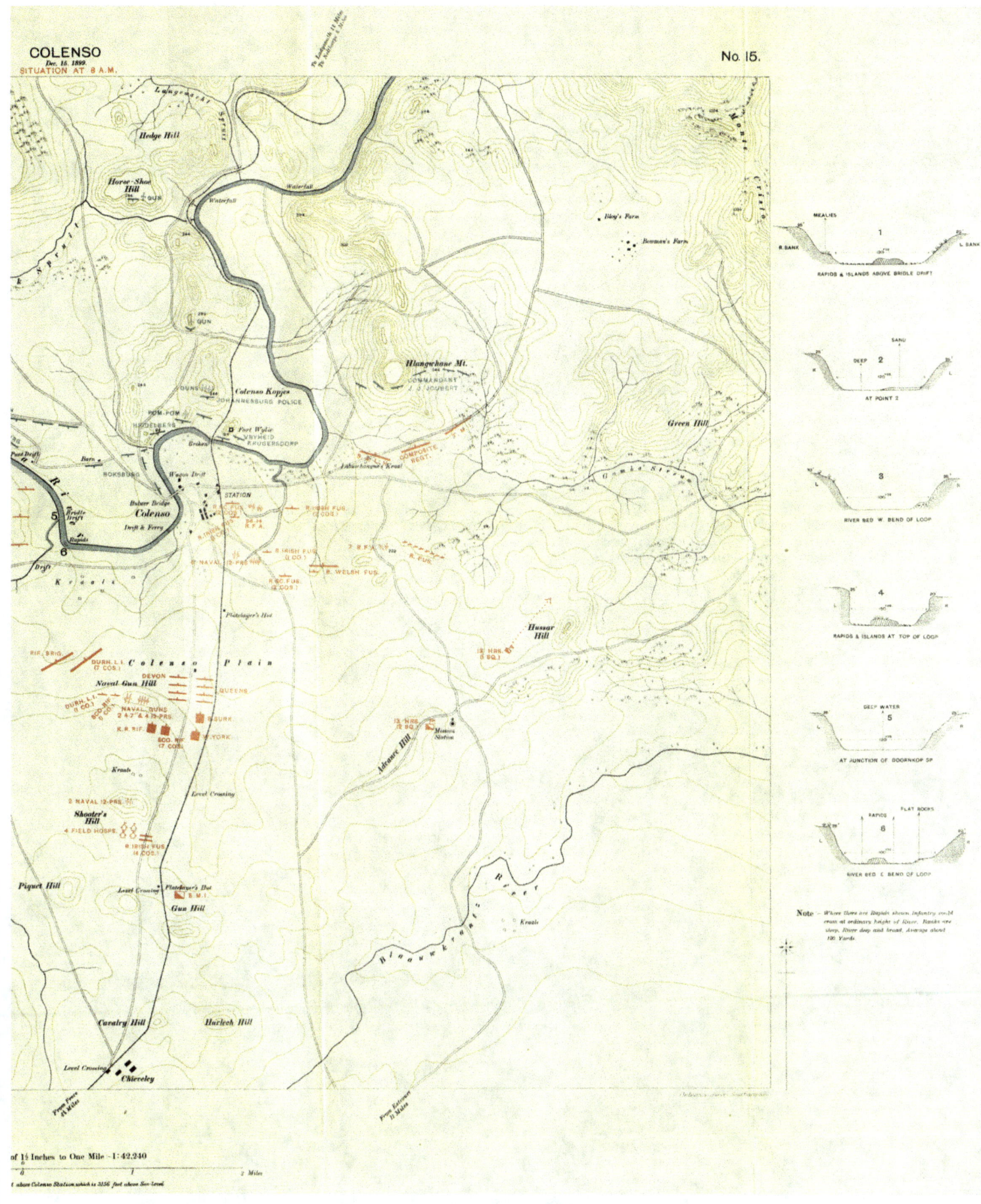

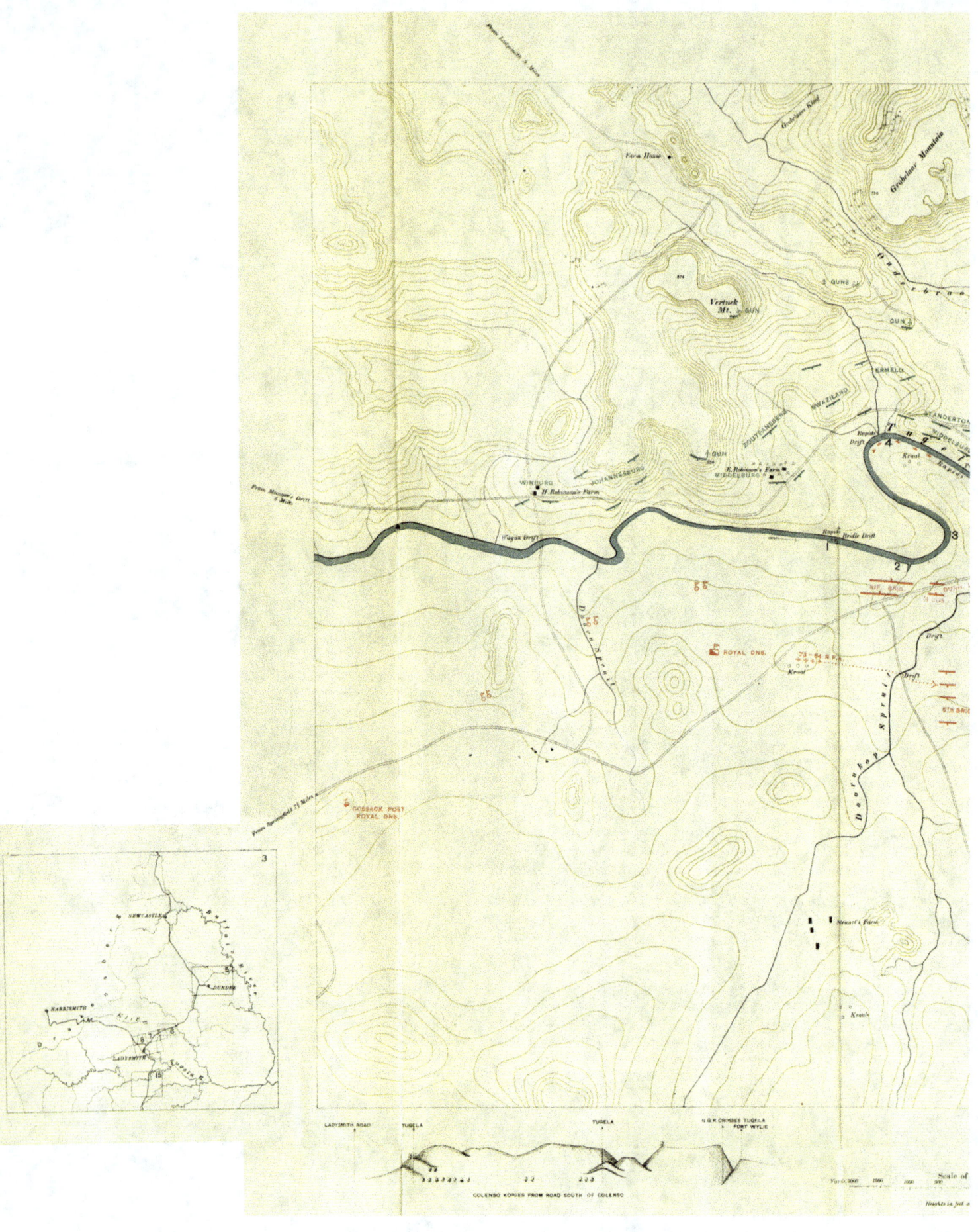

9 [PART OF]
14
16.
BURGERSDORP
MOLTENO
STEYNSBURG
COLESBERG
HAAUWPOORT JUNCTION.
HANOVER
PHILIPSTOWN

From Philipstown 10 Miles
From Petrusville 20 Miles
Fonteintje
Brak Pan
Gras Pan
Bosch Kop
Bochjesman's Hoed
Kraalfontein
Zuig Poort
Leeuwen Berg
Wind Poort
Longwood
Zeekoe Gat R.
Kaffirfontein
Bosch Plaats
Seacow River
Klein Elandsfontein
Flaauw Kop
Drie Koppen
Bas Kop
HANOVER ROAD
Tibbleberg
Dr Dam
Vogelfontein
From Hanover 11 Miles
DWAALFONTEIN
Wildfontein Farm
Steenboks Berg
WILDFONTEIN
Vaschgat Farm
Platjesfontein
Inipers Kop
CARLOSPOORT
Dansters Kop
Honde Kop
Vlagge Kop
Miles 4

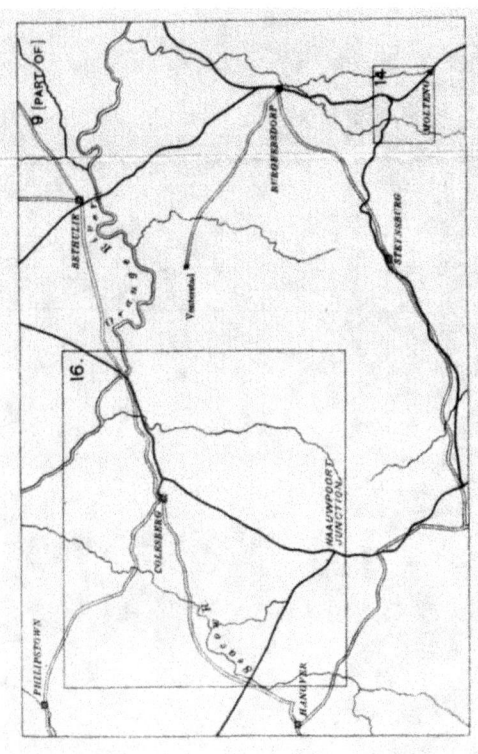

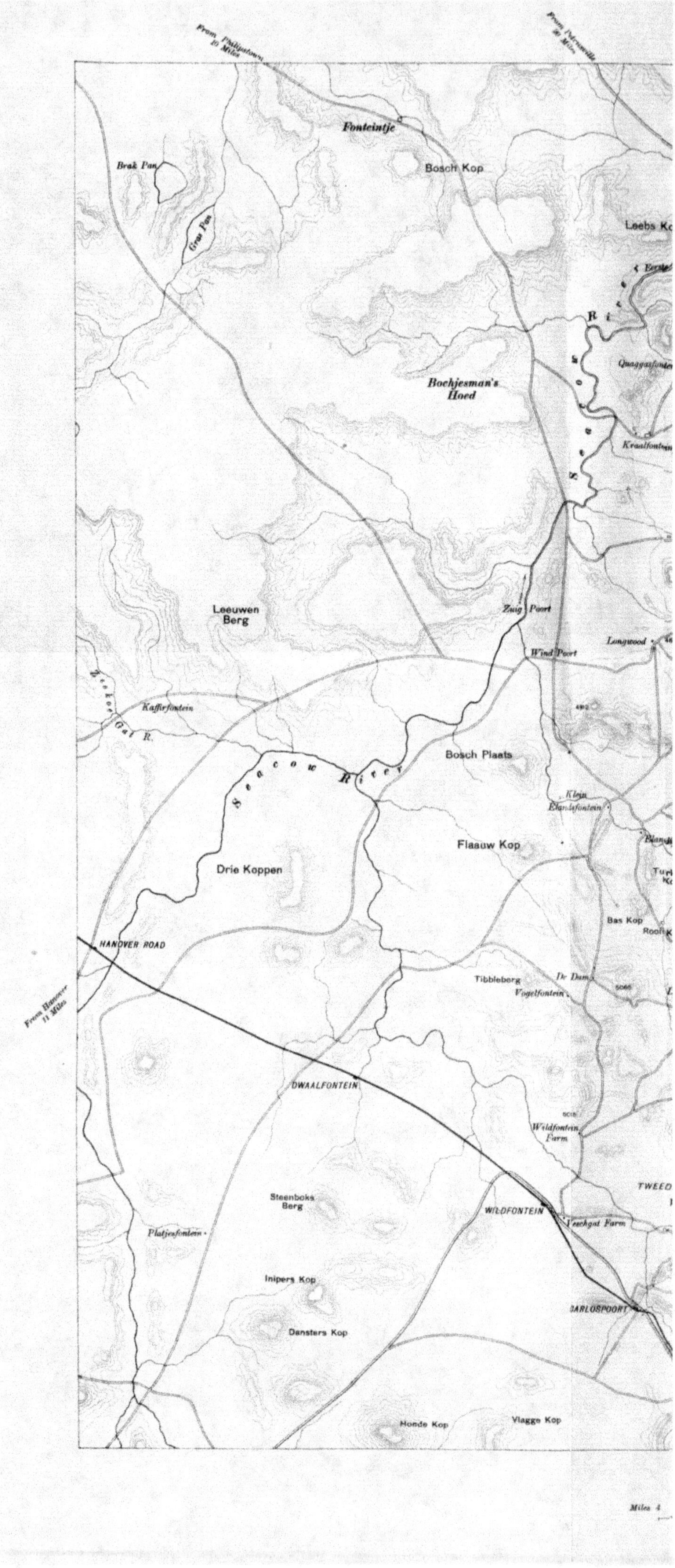

OPERATIONS AROUND COLESBERG

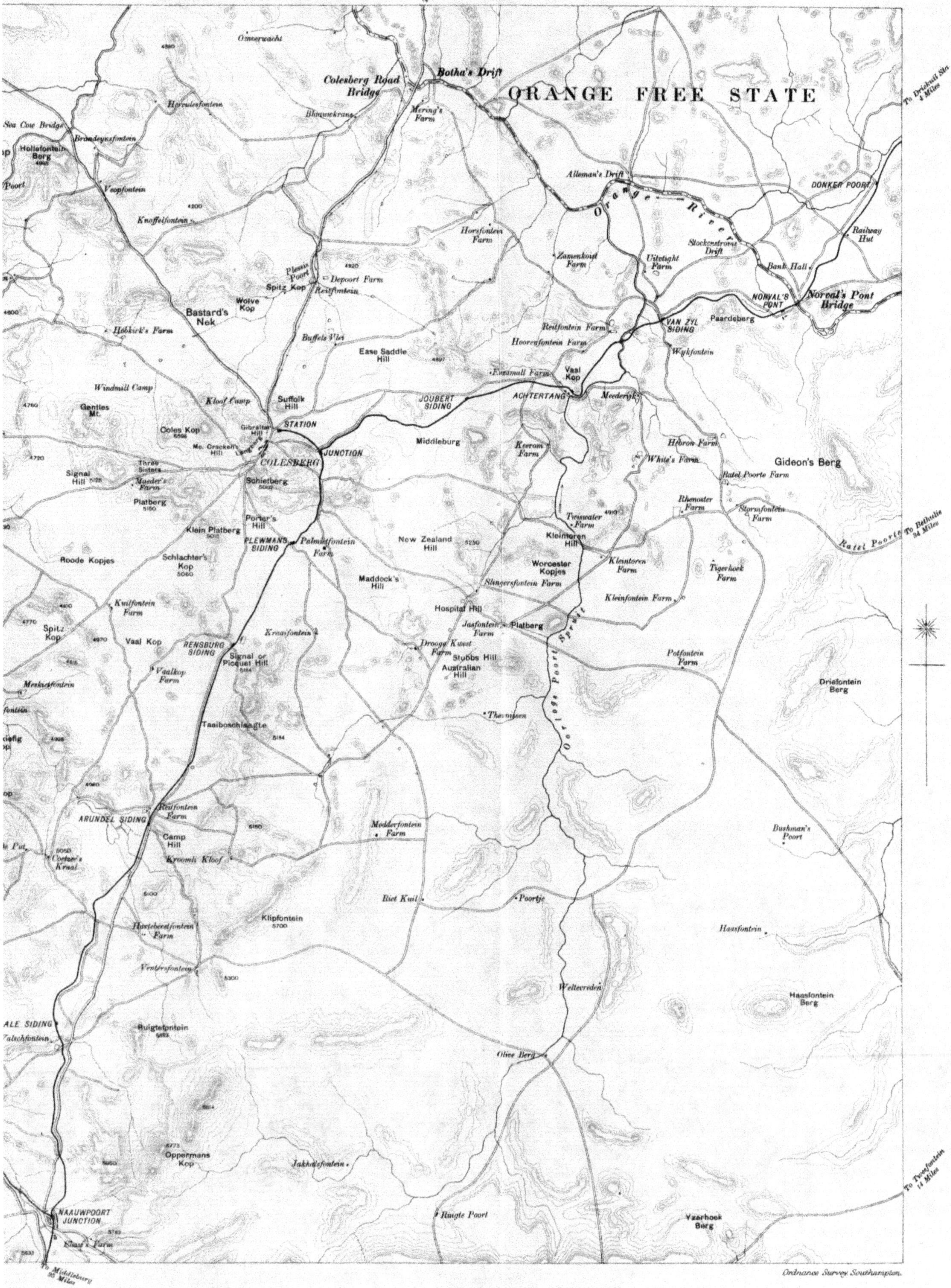

Ordnance Survey Southampton.

Scale of One Inch to Four Miles - 1 : 253,440

3 2 1 0 4 8 12 Miles

Heights in feet above Sea-level

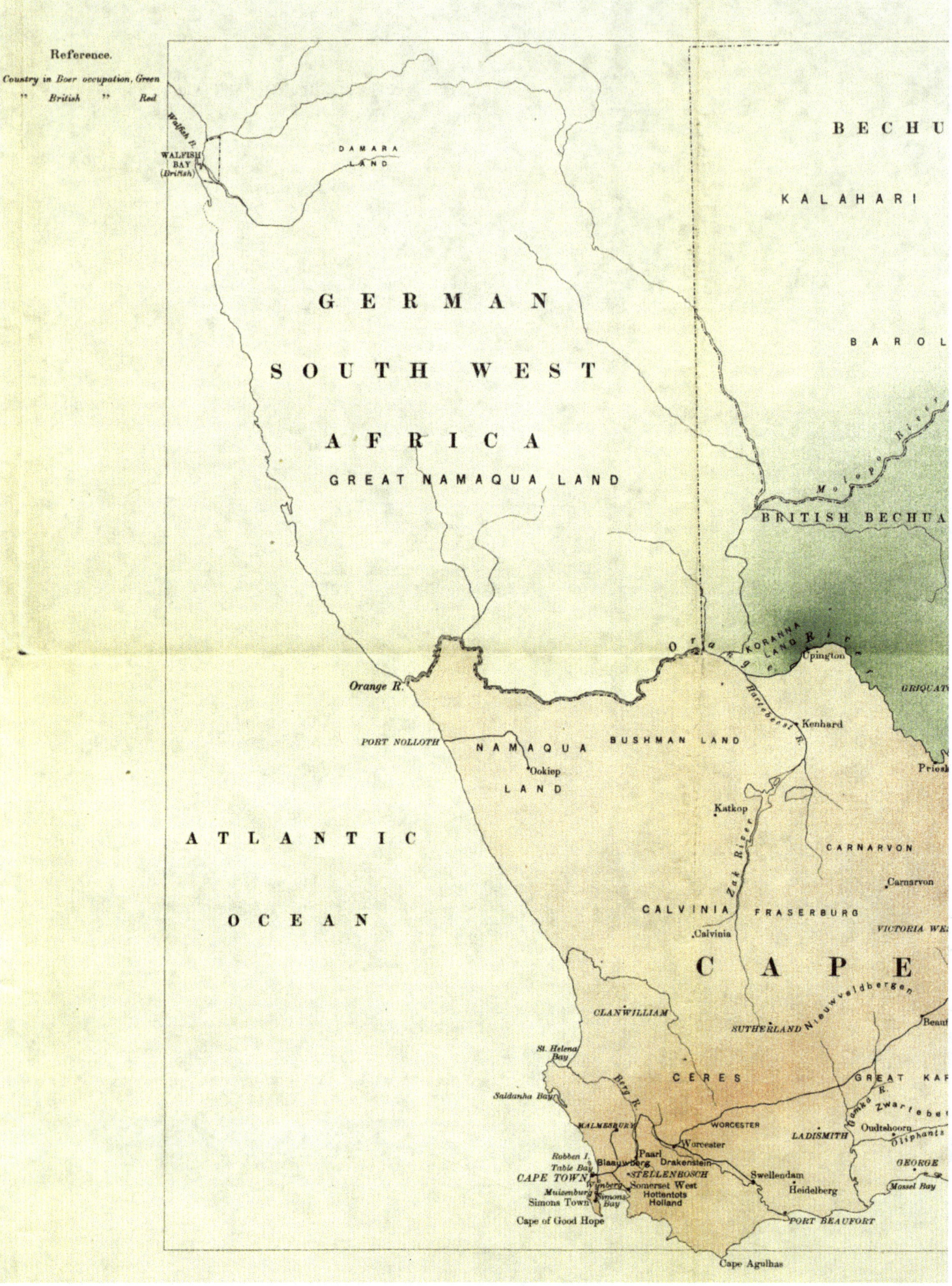

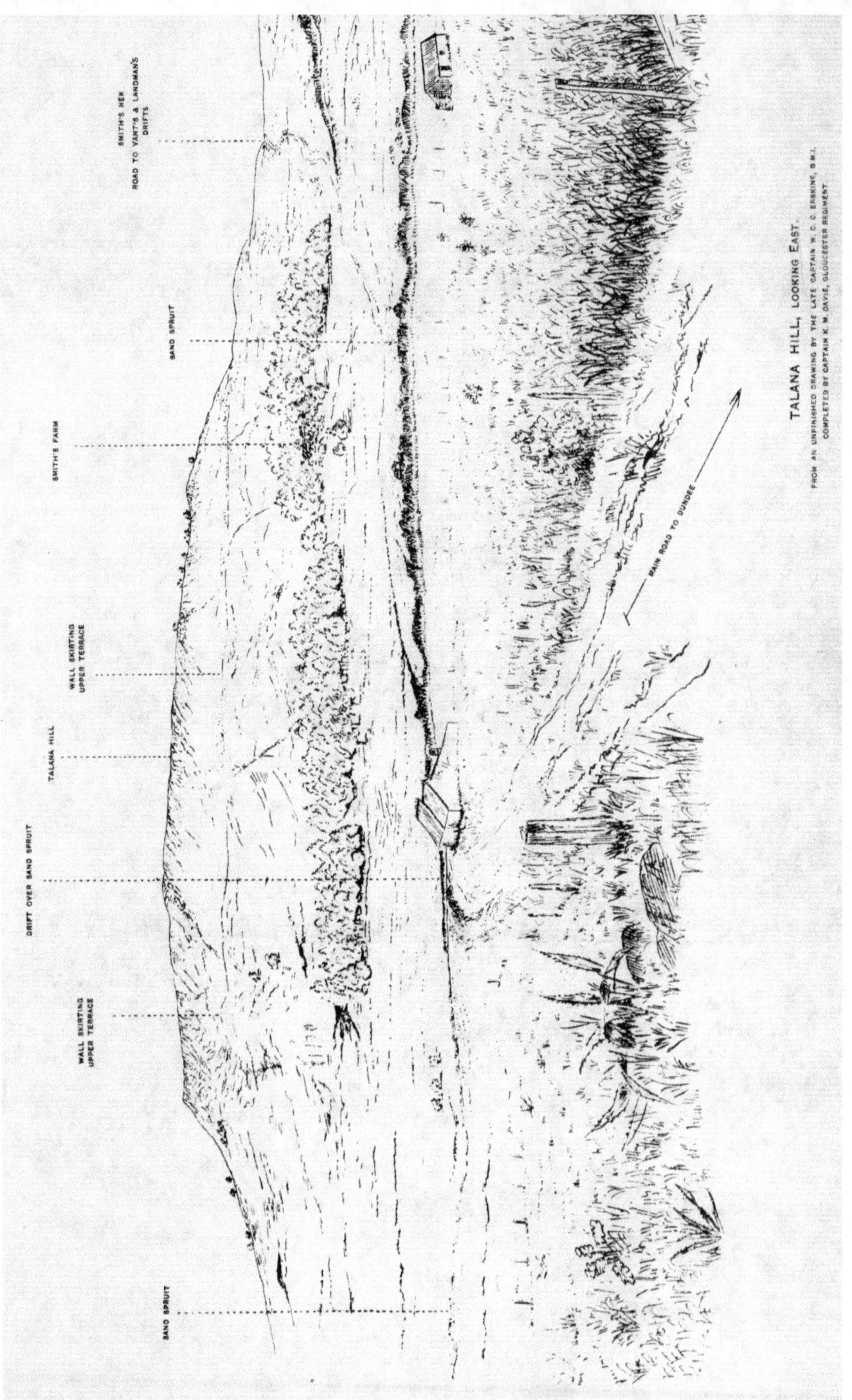

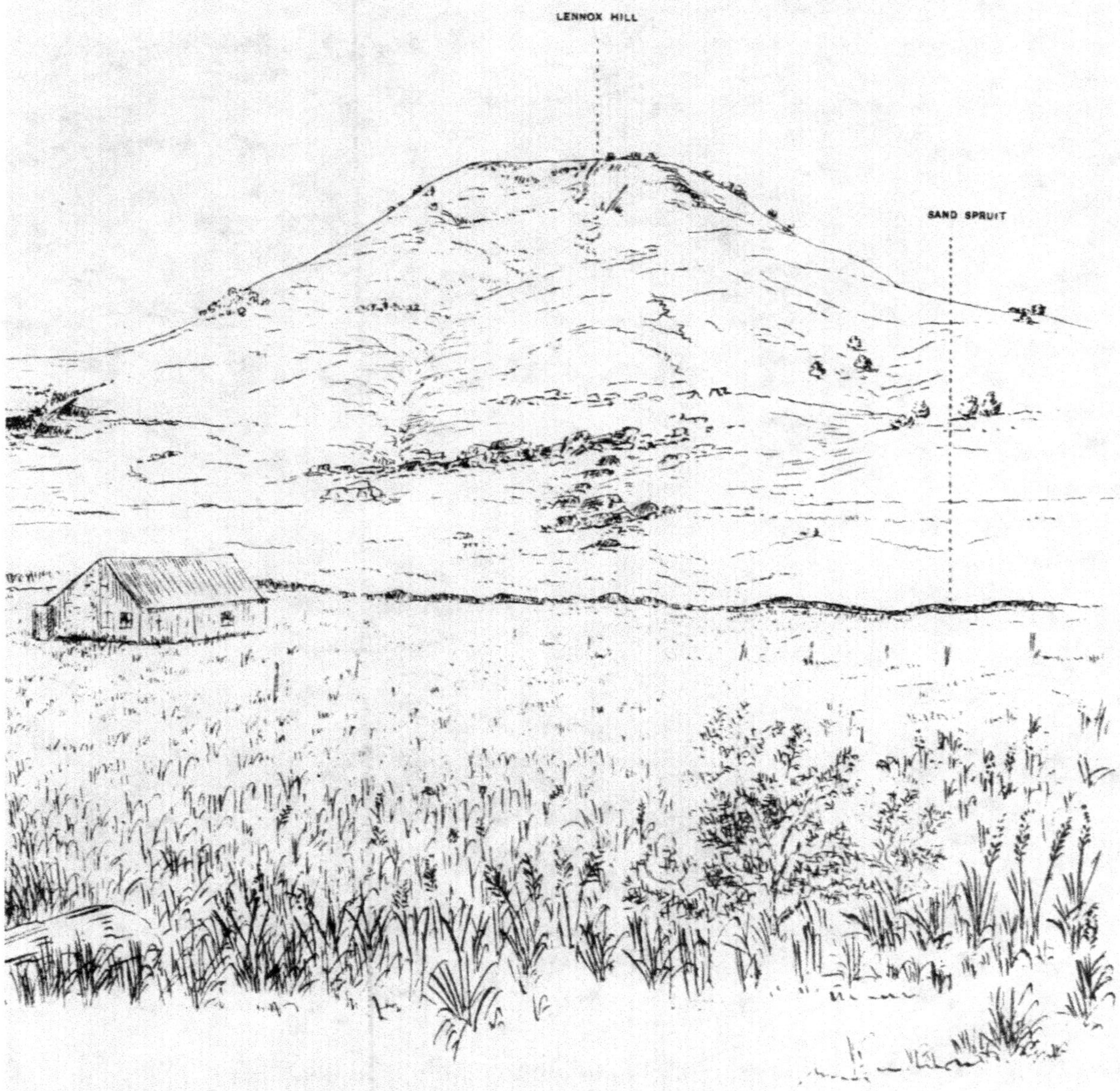

Ordnance Survey, Southampton.

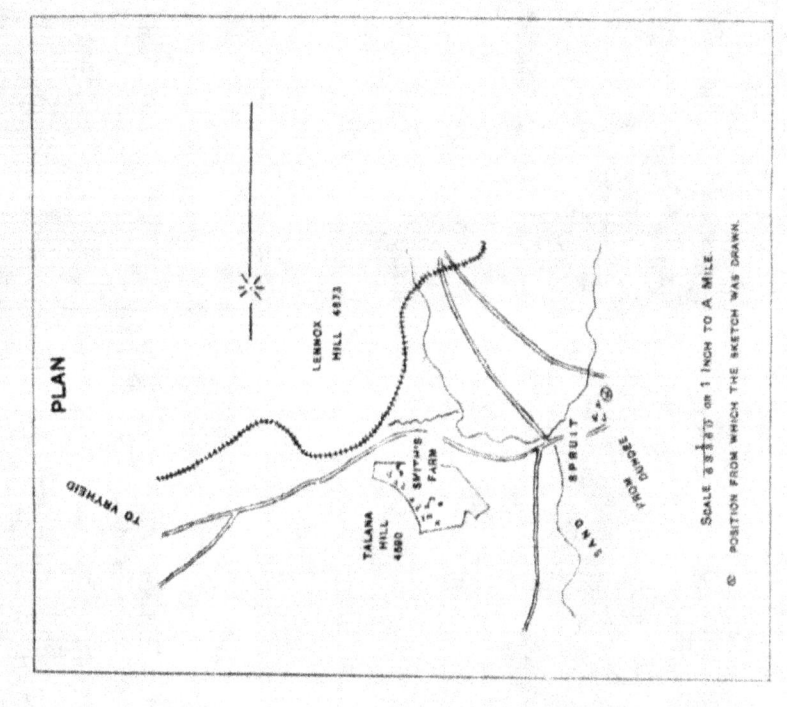

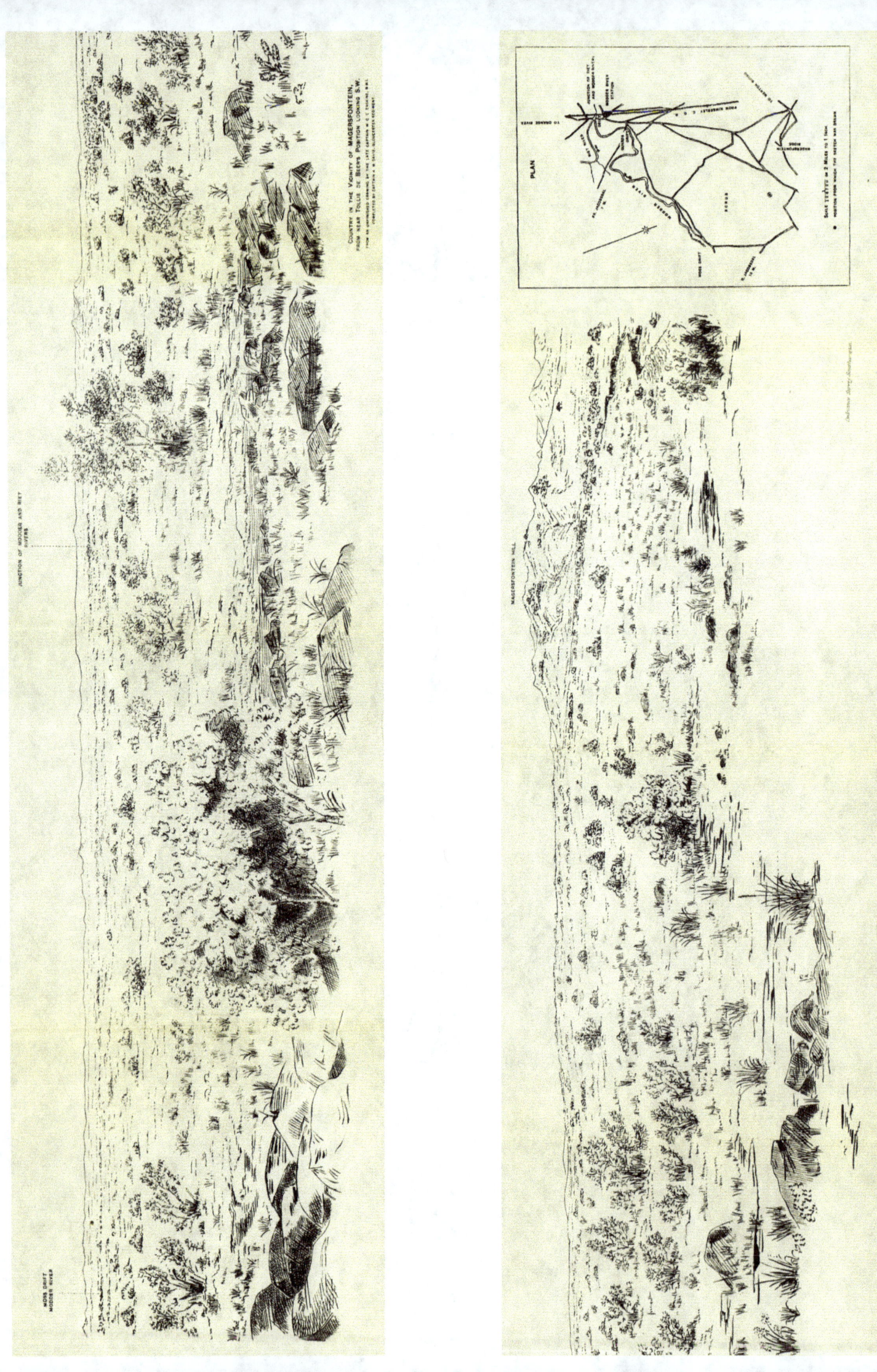

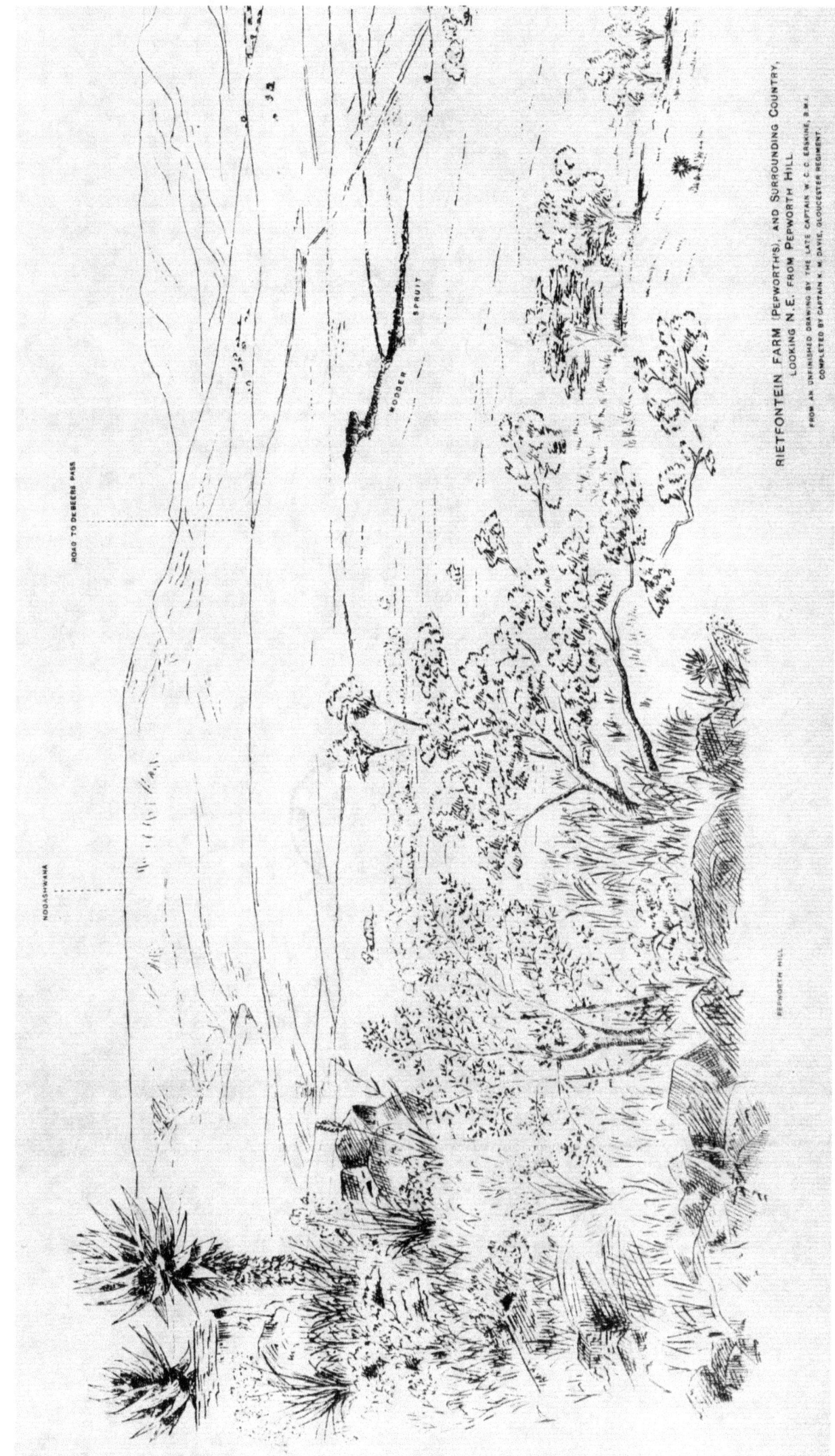

RIETFONTEIN FARM (PEPWORTH'S), AND SURROUNDING COUNTRY, LOOKING N.E. FROM PEPWORTH HILL.

FROM AN UNFINISHED DRAWING BY THE LATE CAPTAIN W. C. C. ERSKINE, R.M.I.
COMPLETED BY CAPTAIN K. M. DAVIE, GLOUCESTER REGIMENT.

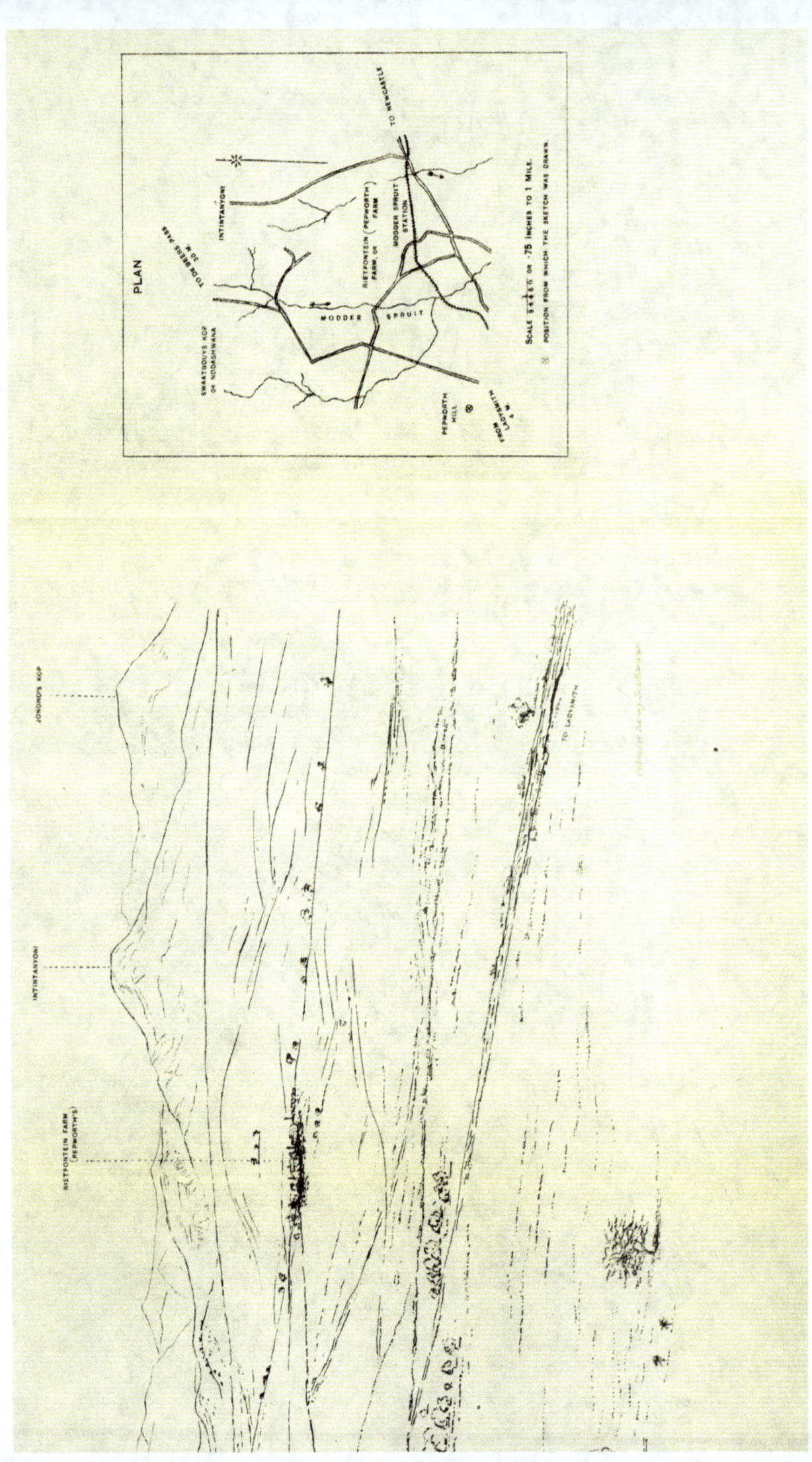

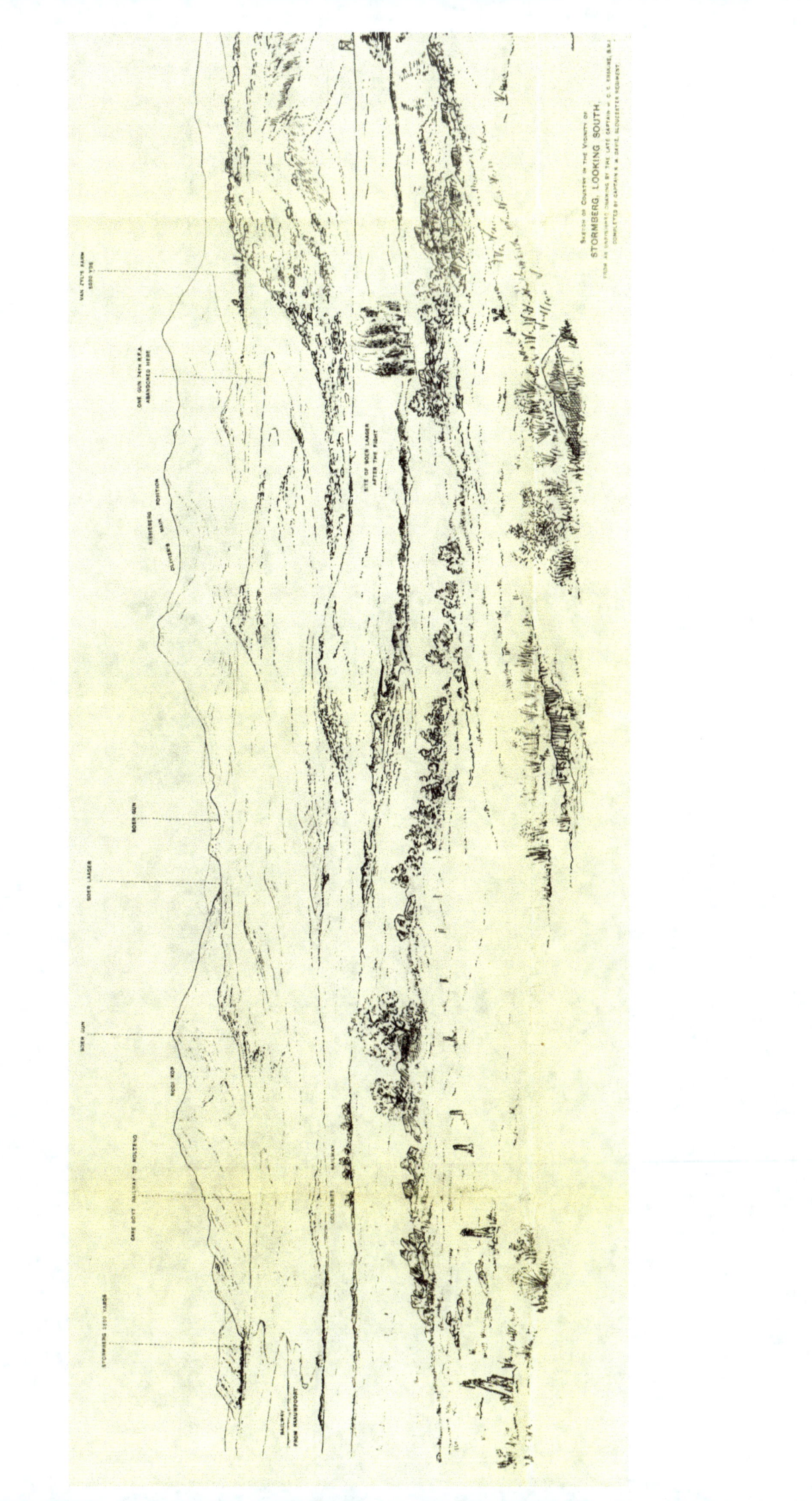

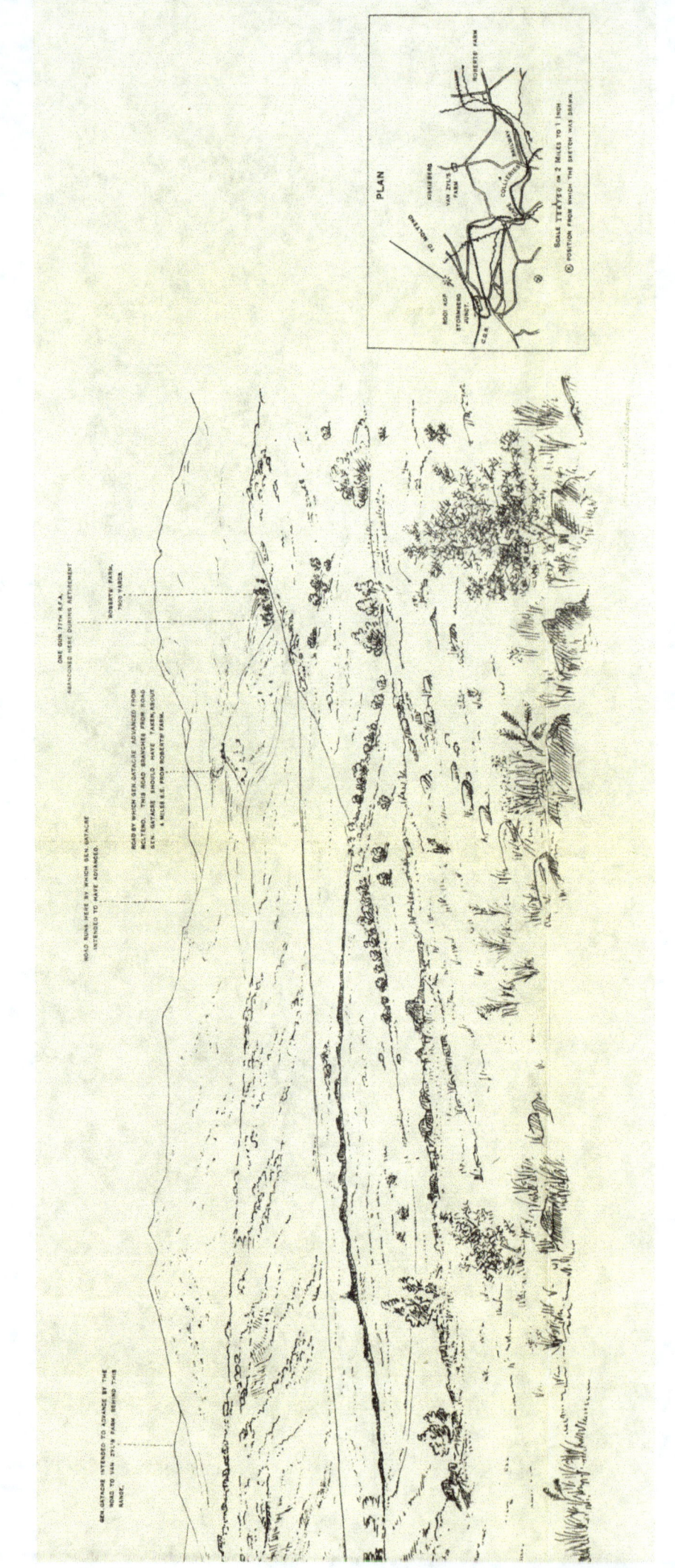

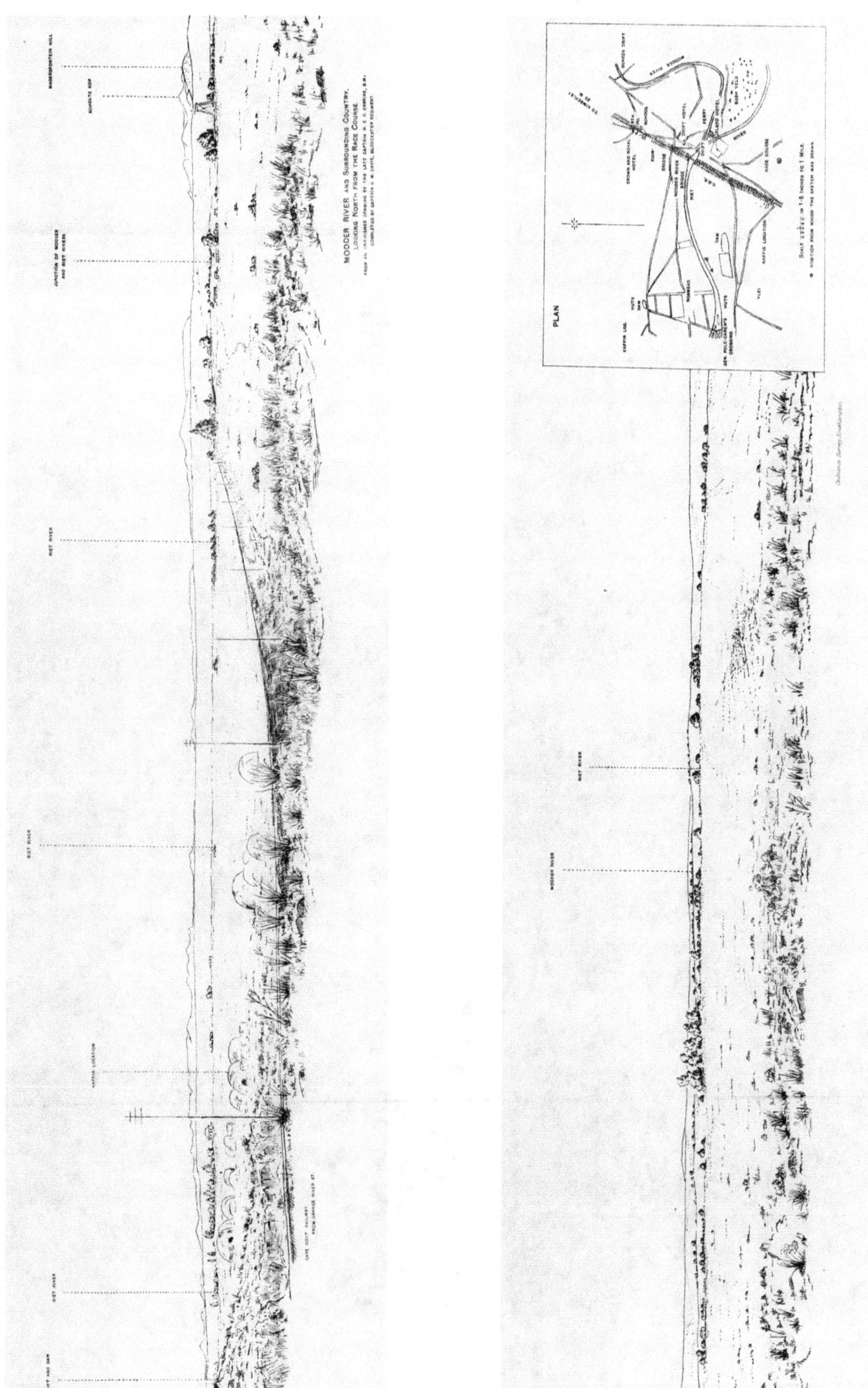

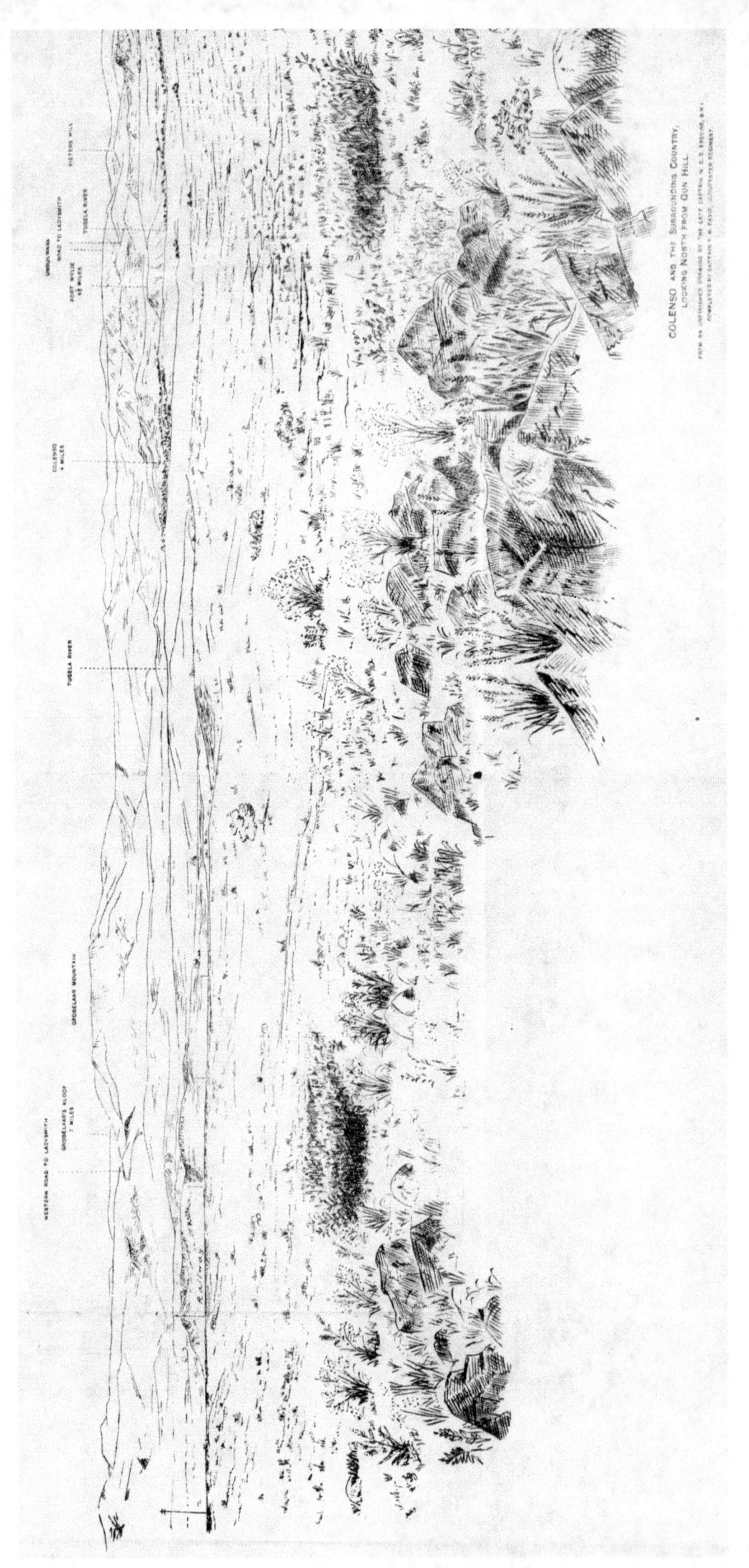